D0850750

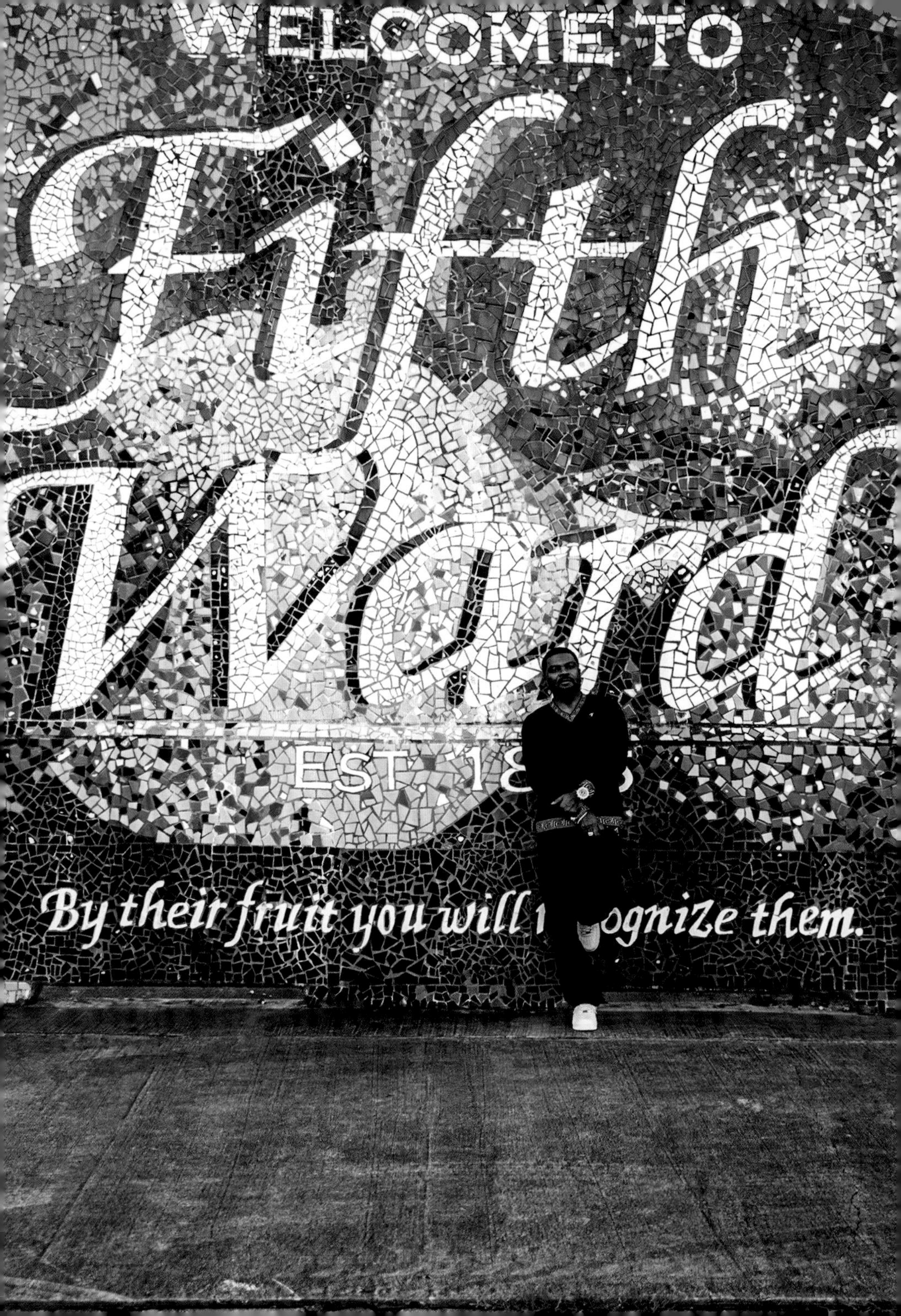
WELCOME TO
Fifth Ward
EST

THE ART & SCIENCE OF

respect

The Art & Science of Respect: A Memoir by James Prince / with Jasmine D. Waters

N-The-Water Publishing
2141 W. Governors Circle
Houston, TX 77092

First N-The-Water Publishing hardcover edition June 2018

The Art & Science of Respect is a registered trademark of N-The-Water Publishing

Publishing Director: Julia Beverly
Editor: Pilar Sanders
Assistant Editors: Maurice G. Garland and Andrew Cencini

Cover Photo: Diwang Valdez
Cover Design: Kevin "Mr. Soul" Harp

Instagram: @JPrinceRespect
Facebook: RapALotRecords
Twitter: @JPrinceRespect

ISBN 978-0-9998370-0-9
ISBN 978-0-9998370-2-3 (ebook)

FOREWORD: RESPECT

Me and my sons Jas and Drake, the first time we brought him down to Houston to ignite the movement.

I honestly don't remember meeting James Prince. It was years ago and a lot of life has happened since then. What I do remember is like scenes from a movie: Being in Houston, on our way to a nightclub, escorted by a motorcade, seas parting everywhere we went, waves, handshakes. All blatant signs of respect and admiration or maybe even fear, to be honest. But it all equaled up to a man straight out of all my favorite movies about power, loyalty, and respect.

My story from *Degrassi* until now has been pretty well-documented. Everyone has heard how Jas Prince found me on Myspace, reached out, brought me to Houston, and introduced me to Lil Wayne. But not much has been said about the things I witnessed from the Prince family during those early years in that city.

There's a common thread throughout the careers of mine and many others, and that is that no one becomes great on our own. Not even me or Pops. Y'know me, Jas, Junior, Baby Jay, those are my brothers, so I call him "Pops." He's a complicated man and it takes time to learn how to read him, even for me.

Through our years he reinforced the importance of being self-contained, how to build a team, and how to respect and value their unconditional support to the movement that you're creating. Our parallels became clearer and clearer. At a time where Toronto was as unlikely to succeed as a former car salesman out of Houston, at a time where rap was either East Coast or West Coast, here we both are. He helped pave the way by building a Third Coast the same way we established the North.

The challenges of creating a movement from scratch are indescribable. Everyone's different and no one has the cheat codes. We're all just feeling our way through, relying on instinct, using whatever tools we've been given. And what James Prince did, from rap to boxing, was build a movement. And he did it for his city.

- Aubrey Drake Graham

PREFACE

It Was Always Houston

THE ART & SCIENCE OF
respect

Sunday, June 15, 2014. As I stood at the center of the Campbell Education Center gym, with my son Jas Prince on my right and Drake on my left, I surveyed the crowd and began to think about how I got here.

My love for Houston, much like my relationship with Hip Hop and boxing, has been a long, stormy ride. I was either in a storm, just got out of a storm, or was on my way to a storm, but no weapons formed against me have prospered.

I was taught that you must believe in something bigger than yourself in order to get something bigger than yourself. For me, that belief was in God and the Fifth Ward. Bound by Buffalo Bayou, Jensen Drive, Liberty Road, and Lockwood, the fifth of Houston's six wards was a den of wolves which raised me to eventually lead the pack. My story is a familiar one: a child raised in a single-parent household. Sometimes we had nothing but street money to keep the lights on.

On this Sunday afternoon during Houston Appreciation Weekend, listening to the cheers of the crowd, I could hear all of the right decisions and all of the wrong ones. Each choice I've made along the way, no matter how controversial, is what led me here.

My work started on the streets of Houston and grew to spawn Rap-A-Lot Records, one of the most profitable independent record labels to date. I've helped develop international superstars like Drake and world champion boxers like Floyd Mayweather and Andre Ward. In the process of becoming a self-made millionaire, I've also landed in the middle of some of the most defining moments of our culture. I tried in vain to save Biggie, a casualty of the East Coast vs. West Coast rap wars. I was one of the first to speak out against the racist censorship of rap music, and the United States government went to war against me, trying to take away the very liberties it promised to offer.

But the story of it all — how I did it, why I did it and what it's ultimately cost me — has never been told. Until now.

I've traveled this planet many times over. I have homes in several cities, including a thousand-acre compound. I own my own private islands. My family is well taken care of and I've employed lifelong friends in legal businesses to keep them off the streets. But light would not exist without darkness, and I've made many sacrifices. It's impossible to build an empire of this magnitude without forgoing business opportunities and sacrificing time with family and friends. At times, it's been necessary to cut people loose.

I'm not a perfect man. My reputation of being ruthless, unforgiving and relentless precedes me. When I believe something has been fore-told by God, I will let no man keep it out of my grasp. So, I begin this story of my life in the spirit of how I've lived it: in brutal, unapolo-getic honesty. What follows are my wins, my losses, and everything I've learned in between.

In hindsight, most people could never have made the decisions I've made, but I challenge you to try and understand them. Everything I did, I did for my family and the Fifth Ward. Whether you're from Houston, Chicago, Toronto or anywhere else, there's a Fifth Ward in every city, in every country, all over this world.

PART ONE:

EVERYTHING BEFORE THAT NIGHT

THE CLOSET

THE ART & SCIENCE OF

respect

I t's the fall of 1988 and I'm sitting on the floor of my bedroom closet with my infant son Jas asleep in my lap. I'm torn. My face is wet from tears and a cold sweat. I know that I'm a walking dead man.

Just outside are the working class streets of the Fifth Ward; secretaries, mechanics, and schoolchildren laughing, going about their daily lives. Where we come from, hope is just a concept. It's an idea that most of us don't share. The focus is on survival, securing a nine-to-five job, just trying to make it home to your family every night. For many of the people I grew up with, that's where the ambition stopped. The idea of *more* just didn't register. But for me, that was all I could think about.

I'm addicted to the pace and sound of the hustle, the luxuries in life and the power that goes along with being able to afford those luxuries. I believe it is always better to have and not need rather than to need and not have. So I became a multi-millionaire as a young adult. I work hard so I can play even harder, on my own terms, on my own time. My goal is to win at everything I do. I've done what I've done to feed my family and to place my children in a better position in life.

Many people start out hustling – whether it's selling drugs, robbing people, or some other illegal hustle – with delusions of grandeur, blind to the inevitable outcome. Not me. I knew the costs of what I was doing. I understood the risk, but I was locked into the streets and I didn't give a damn whether I lived or died. It was all or nothing for me. I knew the consequences of my actions would lead me to one of two places: the penitentiary or a casket. Acutely aware of my fate, I've even calculated possible jail sentences and where I may have to serve them. At any given moment, I'm ready to die. I don't care, and many people hustling with me in the streets share the same mentality. When you're born into poverty, you know that death comes for you first.

At 24, I've already outlived a third of my childhood friends. Because of gun violence and drug abuse, I've attended more funerals than weddings and christenings combined. Half of my surviving associates are behind bars. Just breathing, however heavy, is a risk. But I am immune to the weight of the load. I have to be.

In order to survive the streets, or at least buy yourself a little more time, it's almost as if you have to sell your soul. You trade your feelings, your compassion, and in many ways your humanity for heartlessness. There is no room for emotions. Anything less than savagery can cost you your life. And like I said, I don't care. It's not that I'm afraid to die. I'm not afraid of going to prison either. My biggest fear is knowing all of the money I'll be losing out on.

I put myself in isolation. I've cut off any and everyone capable of making me feel something. My family is kept at arm's length. The irony is in the fact that I'm doing all of this for them, but I'm never comfortable in their presence knowing the things I have to do to provide. My focus remains solely on my one objective: break my family's cycle of poverty. That is my reason for hustling.

I've stopped going to church, something I've done faithfully every Sunday since early childhood. My relationship with God is stronger than anything else in my life. But I can't fake it with Him. I know how I'm living is wrong. And although I'm prepared to die, there is a small part of me that just isn't ready to give up. Instead, I bow my head every morning before finally falling into bed and recite the same prayer: "Before You take my life or lock me up, give me a sign."

There's two ways to reach rock bottom: you can either fall all the way to the bottom, or you can pull the bottom up to you. Either way, on the closet floor, with Jas sleeping in my lap, here it is. Rock bottom.

While I could hear the muffled sounds of the streets out there, in here I can only hear God. This is the sign I've asked for. I've always been the leader of my crew, but they don't know what to make of what is happening to me. And truthfully, neither do I. I've gone from running the streets – and I do mean *running* them – to riding around Houston with a midget rapper.

Rumors run rampant: "He's lost his mind," "He's strung out," "The drugs have finally got him." But aside from trying marijuana once in the fourth grade, I never used drugs. I don't want anything to prevent me from having control over myself. No, I'm not high. In fact, I've never been more sober in my life.

That's the best way to describe this feeling. Sobering. Or better yet, a resurrection. Every part of my estranged humanity is being willed back to life. At this moment, I knew I had to change my life. I didn't want to trade years of balling out in the streets for spending the majority of the rest of my life behind bars. For the first time, I realized that I must break my addiction to the streets if I wanted to have a life of longevity with my family. It's that simple.

I started hustling to make a better situation for my family. More specifically, I wanted to buy my mother a house. But to understand the desperation that fueled that goal, we have to go back to the night I first got the idea.

A VACUUM & A HOUSE

Because of the Arab oil embargo, people were moving to Houston in droves. It was 1975, and the petrol industry was handing out jobs hand over fist. Even if you couldn't get into oil, you could go to outer space every day with NASA at the Lyndon B. Johnson Space Center. The overall feeling throughout Houston was one of abundance. But that feeling of excess, of financial possibilities, of hope, somehow skipped over the Fifth Ward.

I was born James Johnson on Halloween night of 1964 in the Jefferson Davis Hospital; legend has it that the hospital, built on top of a Confederate graveyard, was haunted. My parents, Sharon Smith and Adam Hackett, were both teenagers. I was Sharon's second child and Adam's first. By the time I could walk, I was living in the Fifth Ward. By age 8 I was in the Cleme Manor Housing apartments, known affectionately (or not) as Coke Street.

Life in public housing is what you might imagine. On the inside, it's a community based on family, faith, and just getting by. You know your neighbors and all of their business, and they know all of yours. Every day is another day in the struggle. From the outside looking in, it's a world of chaos. To them it might be "black on black crime," but to us, it might be one of your lifelong neighbors cheating another neighbor in a card game. That's the thing about the hood; it's filled with ordinary people making everyday decisions based on only what they can see. Not statistics. People.

Growing up in poverty means becoming acquainted with the struggle. Things like gang violence, hunger, evictions, and relatives coming and going to the penitentiary are not news headlines. They're normal occurrences. It's enough to dull your senses. You're exposed to many stresses of adulthood long before you're old enough to understand them. That's one of the main differences between the lower and upper class: time.

The middle class often protects their children by shielding them from what adulthood may bring, allowing them time to grow and mature as people. The impoverished protect their children by exposing them to everything as early as possible, to prepare them for life. That difference in time, so early in our lives, affects how well we'll move throughout the rest of our days.

Growing up, I felt like death was always around me. It seemed like every other week I was being dragged into another funeral. Cousins, neighbors, friends of the family, it was an endless sea of death. I dreaded it. Even under the calmest circumstances, funerals were always a show. I've seen it all: People weeping in the aisles, throwing themselves in the casket, trying to pull the body out of the casket, even threatening to jump into the open grave so they wouldn't have to live their lives in grief. I was too young to understand that type of pain. It didn't register that loss could make you do such things. All I knew was that death was a traumatizing thing and that it was everywhere I turned.

My older sister Zenia Johnson and I were typical siblings. Zenia was a year older than me and could be bossy one minute and playmate the next, just like every other big sister. Our rooms were side by side on Coke Street, while my mother worked hourly jobs doing everything from waiting tables to managing an aquarium warehouse. My sister and I would walk home from school, do chores, do our homework, play outside with our friends, eat whatever our mother cooked, get ready for bed and do it all over again the next day. Our grandmother, Vera Johnson, lived a few miles away and we'd shuffle between the two houses, playing the entire trip. That was our life.

In December of 1976, on a random weeknight, instead of going to bed at our normal 9 PM curfew, Zenia and I stayed up. We laid in our rooms past midnight, just talking. This was a first for us. At twelve and eleven, respectively, we'd both finally reached an age where we could appreciate each other's thoughts. We talked about the future, something I thought a lot about. Even at eleven years old, I had a clear interest in one thing: money. I told my sister about my plans to amass a fortune by becoming a professional football player.

I was in the little league; fast enough, but no one would call me a stand-out athlete. Nevertheless, my plan was to go pro. I'd seen OJ Simpson in the *JET* Magazine and was mesmerized by his lifestyle. But more than anything, I identified with his success story. I thought, *I want to have money like him*. Zenia and I were incredibly different, which was evident by our individual answers to the same question: "What are you going to buy mama when we get grown?"

My sister was practical. Her plan was to get a steady job and buy our mother a vacuum cleaner. As the oldest, Zenia was responsible for the bulk of the household chores. Money was always tight and we couldn't afford a vacuum cleaner, so much of her time was spent sweeping up the house. So her gift to our mother would be a vacuum cleaner. I declared that I would buy our mother a house.

The next morning we'd wake as usual, get dressed and prepare to leave for school. Zenia kissed our mother, as I did. Then Zenia turned to kiss me goodbye. The last thing any eleven year old boy wants is a kiss from his sister. But maybe it was our late night talk just hours before, or maybe she just caught me off guard. Whatever the reason, I allowed my sister to give me a kiss on the cheek. We said goodbye and she was out the door.

Hours later I was at football practice, working on my dream of going pro, when a few local kids came running onto the field, yelling, "Your sister just got hit by a train!"

By the time I got down to the train tracks, halfway between our grandmother's house and the Coke apartments, there were people everywhere. At first, I didn't want to believe it. It wasn't registering to me that Zenia, my sister, could've been hit. Kids were retelling what they'd seen. Accounts of her leg, separated from her body, jumping around on its own. The noise was deafening. I didn't think it was true until I saw the coat, the same ratty coat she'd worn all fall and into the chilly Houston winter. Only this time it was stained in red, with chunks of my sister tangled within it.

This was 1976, a long time before cell phones. Standing there at the train tracks, watching everyone yell and scream in morbid excitement around remnants of my sister, the only thing I wanted was to talk to my mother.

Zenia was in a coma. She had crossed the tracks on the way home from school when she was hit. We all crossed those tracks every day. The train cut her in half. My mother insisted she'd be okay, but she never regained consciousness.

Zenia was declared dead four days later. I remember walking into the church feeling different. This wasn't just another funeral. My sister's father and his family were there. All my aunts, uncles, cousins, and many of my classmates gathered around. There were tears and theatrics. But instead of feeling scared as I normally did at funerals, this time I felt nothing but pain.

That night I went home to Coke Street and I couldn't sleep. I couldn't turn the lights off. I couldn't think. I couldn't lay still. It didn't feel like home anymore. It was just an empty reminder of just how painful life could be, of how everything can change in the blink of an eye. I kept thinking about our last night together, about our talk of the future. We were so certain of what life would be like, of who we would become. Only as I laid there now, the room still and empty, I knew that we'd only been guessing. I had no idea what was in store for me.

That night, at eleven years old, I realized I'd have to buy my mother both the vacuum cleaner and the house.

I didn't sleep for days following Zenia's death. I couldn't. I was haunted. My dead sister would come to me in my dreams. Only now, she was whole again. I could see her smile, hear her voice. It was as if she wanted to remain with me like everything was alright, when it wasn't. She would talk to me, like we did during out last night together. Everything was present and future tense. Her spirit felt so real, her presence felt so strong, that all I could do was wait for sunrise.

The terror from those sleepless nights quickly spread into the rest of my young life. I began falling asleep in class. I was withdrawn from my friends. Depression was setting in and I knew if something didn't change I wasn't going to be able to hold on much longer.

So, at eleven years old, I made the second most important decision of my young life. I asked my mother if I could go live with my grandmother. If I had stayed in that house, surrounded by the memory of my sister and visited nightly by her spirit, I would've wasted away.

People aren't meant to live in one moment, even if that moment is beautiful or the next moment is scary. I had to get out. My mother was working still, doing the best she could to support her youngest child while mourning her eldest. Even in her deepest despair, she made sure we had food on the table, clean clothes on our backs and a roof over our heads. But she didn't know what to do for my ailing spirit.

So, I chose to save myself. And from the moment I arrived at my grandmother's house, I knew I'd made the right decision.

A SPIRITUAL JOURNEY

THE ART & SCIENCE OF
respect

The most important decision of my life involved getting on a city bus. Growing up, there were many things my mother couldn't give me. She'd dropped out of high school to work full-time and take care of my older sister and myself. Years later I learned that she was pregnant with a little boy no more than a year after I was born. He was stillborn, the cord wrapping around his neck during delivery. For my mother, life was a constant set of challenges with limited resources. But the one thing she was able to give me was God.

Every Sunday a bus would ride through the Coke Street Housing Projects and pick up anyone willing to get on. This was a gift to my mother which she passed on to me. Each week she would walk my sister and I out to the corner and put us on it. She didn't have to worry about our safety because the bus only had one destination. And from the moment we got on it until the moment we returned home, we were under the care of Pastor C.L. Jackson of the Pleasant Grove Baptist Church.

Pleasant Grove Baptist Church still stands on Conti Street, about a ten-minute ride from Coke Street. But for me, as a young child, those ten minutes were the difference between the hell of poverty and the heaven of faith. My connection to God began as a connection to C.L. Jackson. He was a tenth grade drop-out, but he was an intelligent and genuine man who was able to make the idea of God digestible to a child. When he spoke, I listened. When he taught me why prayer was important, I understood. And when he told me that God would take care of me, I believed him.

Like most Black Baptist churches, the choir was an important part of the ministry. All week long I'd fuss and fight my way through life just to get to church on Sunday. I started to look forward to it. Service was relief and the choir was the warm honey my spirit needed. The music would touch me to the point where I'd find myself singing the hymns during the week when I needed something to soothe me. My mother was working a lot and rarely home, leaving my sister and I to fend for ourselves. Often we'd go hungry. I'd walk around the neighborhood in tears, singing, "Lord do it, Lord do it. Do it for me right now," letting the word help stave off my hunger until my mother made it home.

After my sister died and I moved to my grandmother's house, I was so full of conviction that I made the single most important decision of my life. I was no longer living in the projects, so there was no church bus every week. But I needed to be close to the Lord. By then, church had become a regular part of my life. I couldn't even imagine my week without it. So one Sunday morning, at eleven years old, I got myself up, got dressed, went out to the corner and paid ten cents to catch the city bus to church. I've done a lot in my life, much of which I'll share in the pages to come. But no single act is more defining of who I am as a person than that moment right there. I am willing to do whatever it takes to get what I need.

My relationship with God was strengthened through Pleasant Grove and would only grow stronger throughout the rest of my life. My faith gave me a moral compass; direction in a world of chaos. And because of it, I was always able to stay on course even when everyone around me appeared lost. Believing in something bigger than myself brought me comfort and added purpose to my life. When you're acting within your purpose, with your divine conviction, nothing can stop you.

Even though we didn't have a lot of material things, my family always had my back. Through the years I've seen that if push came to shove, I wasn't shoving alone. My family has gone to war with me and for me, and that is an amazing feeling. Now imagine that feeling multiplied by a million. God is the reason I move without fear, the reason I've been able to take the risks I've taken. I've seen moments that defied any explanation other than God's grace and mercy.

But faith alone is not enough. Right now, if you travel through any housing projects in America, I guarantee you'll find some of God's strongest believers. Life in general – but especially for the impoverished and disenfranchised – is far too hard to do alone. Each day holds a promise of hope or despair and often times a little bit of both. While I've come to trust in "God's will be done," I've also come to understand that faith without works is dead. I would not be where I am today without God and without the work ethic that God allowed my family to instill in me.

Believing is not enough. I've seen miracles, but I don't wait on them. Just as I had to make a decision to move to my grandmother's instead of rotting in my mother's grief-stricken apartment, or getting up on a Sunday morning while everyone else slept and taking the city bus to go hear the Word, I had to make a decision that I was going to lift myself out of poverty. I knew there was something more than the life in front of me. I knew there was a much bigger world out there. I knew it because I'd seen it on a ride to prison.

ESCAPE TO THE PENITENTIARY

THE ART & SCIENCE OF *respect*

There are 65.9 miles between Houston and Huntsville, Texas. That's a little over an hour drive; however, in my grandmother's car, it was more like a two-hour drive since she didn't move that fast. These trips helped set the course of my life.

My uncle, Lonzell Johnson, known to us as "Hamp," was incarcerated for most of my childhood. Unfortunately, this wasn't unusual for an African-American male. The penitentiary is so ingrained in our lives that many of us approach the possibility of incarceration not as *if* but as *when*. To understand the gravity of this, you have to truly wrap your mind around the idea of being housed in a box. A literal cage. That is what life is like for millions of men and women in this country, living as caged animals. And while some of them truly are a threat to society, there are far more locked up for drug addictions; they're only a threat to themselves. My uncle Hamp was locked up for burglary. Routinely, I'd get into my grandmother's late model Ford Taurus and we'd drive the two hours to see him.

Thankfully, I've never had to visit any of my children in prison, so I can only imagine the pain my grandmother felt driving those long hours to see her only son. For me, the trip was something totally different. In a bizarre irony, the trip to the penitentiary was nothing short of a vacation for me. It was my chance to get out of the hood, to see the world; to encounter people who didn't look like me, sound like me, or experience the world the same way I did. And most importantly, those road trips exposed me to land.

I was always outdoorsy. I loved to hunt and fish. I'd swim in the summer, up until the day I almost drowned at the pool across from Coke Street. And of course, I kept my chickens and roosters outside. But I hadn't really seen the country outside of Houston until we began taking those journeys to Huntsville. We'd ride for hours looking at nothing but lush green grass, thousands of trees, my world expanding with each mile. The bookends of my trip - the ghetto and the prison - were nothing compared to the endless possibilities of who I could become in between. Land became important. It represented peace, space to do something with my life, and ownership.

It was during one of these trips that I said, "Grandma, I'm going to own some land like this one day." My grandmother just looked at me like I was crazy. I was only nine years old then, but the seeds of success had already been planted. That's what many people never understand. Failure has birthed far more champions than privilege. I am the man I am today not just because of what I had early in life but also because of what I *didn't* have.

Looking back on it now, I understand how important it is for every child, not just the impoverished, to travel outside of their surroundings. Those trips taught me perspective and exposed me to how other people lived; it expanded my goals. I didn't just want to buy my mother a house. Now I wanted to buy her some land with a home on it.

I had even larger dreams for myself. I didn't just want to own a few acres. I wanted to own more land than the eye could see. I wanted to own enough land to make sure the space between the hood and the penitentiary was wider than I'd ever be able to cross in my lifetime.

ERNEST & ADAM

THE ART & SCIENCE OF

respect

People in the South are often exposed to sex at younger ages. Perhaps that's because there's less distractions in rural areas, or because we get married at younger ages. Or perhaps there's a greater emphasis on family, and settling down sooner, so you're more aware of it. I'm sure the oversexualization of African-Americans during the slave trade also plays a large part in the complex and often contradictory attitude towards sex in the South. And these contradictions often affect the most vulnerable among us: rapes and molestations often go unreported or unpunished. Many of these things that are common today were taboo enough in the 1960s to leave you socially ostracized or even killed. Sex was the one thing everyone did, but no one knew how to talk about it properly.

Sharon Johnson was at work at Big J's Bowling Alley the night Adam Hackett and Ernest Prince walked in. She noticed nothing out of the ordinary about the two best friends. They sat in her section and made small talk as she took their order. Sharon was fifteen and already the mother of a three-month-old girl, Zenia. The relationship between Sharon and her daughter's father was over, and her focus was on adjusting to life as a teenage mother. She'd just returned to high school and was determined to finish – something that no one in her family had been able to accomplish. Her mother Vera wasn't particularly happy about Sharon's pregnancy, but was committed to helping raise her grandchild as long as Sharon held down a job.

One night in the fall of 1963, Sharon saw Adam Hackett again. She was hanging out with her friend Anna Marie at Julia C. Hester House, a local community center that threw dances for area teens in hopes of keeping them off the streets and out of trouble. Sharon and Anna Marie were neighbors. Like most teenage girls, they were into music, hanging out with their friends, and talking to young men. Ernest Prince struck up a conversation with Anna Marie, and Adam took a liking to Sharon. That night would be the start of a lifelong bond between the four of them. Adam and Sharon began dating. Adam's family wasn't happy that he was dating a girl with a baby, but Adam didn't seem to mind, often spending time with young Zenia.

Adam was born in Louisiana in 1944. The second oldest of nine children, he was a straightforward guy from a hard-working family, who always held down at least one job. His father was stern - some might even say mean - which made him hard to live with. So Adam, who never had less than two jobs, moved out on his own at seventeen years old, renting an apartment with his best friend Ernest. He loved Sharon and when she became pregnant in January of 1964, Adam was supportive, eagerly awaiting the birth of his first child. By this time, Adam had fallen out with Ernest and moved in with his sister. Still, Sharon visited often as their love for one another grew.

On Halloween morning, 1964, Sharon was at home when she began having pains. Her cousin drove her to Jefferson Davis Hospital where she was checked out and sent home. She was in labor but not far enough along. A few hours later, while experiencing more powerful contractions, Sharon caught the bus by herself and returned to the hospital, only to be released an hour later. Finally, Sharon was in her mother's bed that evening when her water broke. She was admitted to the hospital shortly before I was born. Adam arrived some time later, overjoyed to meet his son.

Houston was experiencing a bitter cold spell, and Vera's house was out of gas. Fourteen-month-old Zenia was sent to stay with her father's family while Sharon and her newborn son, which was me, left the hospital headed for my Aunt Teddy's. There was an adjustment period. Sharon now had two children at sixteen, and Adam had a family to provide for. But they did the best they could for a while before breaking up; Sharon returned to her mother's house, although she continued dating Adam off and on for many years to come.

The separation never stopped Adam from being present in my life; he still made sure I spent time with my grandparents, aunts, uncles and cousins. I was loved and treated like everyone else in the family. Only, there was one thing. Anna Marie, my mother's best friend, began commenting on how much I favored her ex-boyfriend Ernest. I was small with dark brown skin and a thin, muscular frame. My mother dismissed the remarks. She said I looked just like Adam, and made sure Anna Marie never said anything around me.

I was in the ninth grade when I met Sheldon Harris and her cousin Ronda Prince, who were a few years younger than me. They were cute little girls and I wanted to talk to them both, but I ended up talking to Sheldon. She had long pretty hair and a sweet smile, and she liked me, too. We'd walk home after school and talk on the phone, and eventually she asked for a picture of me so she could show her mother. I obliged, because at that point I was going to do anything Sheldon asked me to do. I liked her that much. That night she called me, and I heard her mother in the background saying, "That boy looks exactly like Ernest Prince."

Ernest was Ronda's daddy, but I knew him as someone who occasionally hung around my mother. Of course I told my mother what she said and she dismissed it. "Adam Hackett is your father," she said, and then she ended the conversation. It wasn't something that stuck with me at the time. For thirteen years I had no reason to doubt that Adam was my daddy. But later that year, in the summer, my mother took me to the Prince family reunion.

Family reunions are a big deal, especially in the South. Relatives from all over the world gather together for days of fellowship and barbecue. It's not uncommon to invite family friends to join the camaraderie. But imagine walking into a house full of people who all look exactly like you. I didn't know what to make of it. Everyone was welcoming, friendly, and treated me like any other guest. But that night, as I returned to my grandmother's house, I was confused. Angry. It felt like a funeral was happening inside of me. That's the best way to describe it; it felt like death.

Still, my mother denied that Ernest was my father. It wasn't so much that she was trying to deceive me; she was trying to protect me. I loved Adam, and Adam loved me. Our bond as father and son was as strong as any other family. But the sense of doubt growing inside me made me feel like our bond was slowly dying. I was losing that sense of security, of identity, and no amount of reassurance from my mother could bring it back. It changed me. It's a heck of a thing to question your own paternity. It's not something I'd wish on my worst enemy. As a child, your first basic knowledge of yourself is your name, and the name of your mother and father. Now, my father's name was followed by a question mark. Whether my mother knew it or even wanted to admit it, that night after the family reunion, I knew Adam Hackett wasn't my blood daddy.

Ernest Prince was fearless. The third of nine children, he had a natural finesse about him. A natural born leader, he always had a crew and a girlfriend. He'd even dated one of his teachers in high school and wasn't afraid of getting caught; he was only afraid she'd get too attached. He was a natural wanderer. In the ninth grade Ernest went to New York to live with his older brother Donald. Ernest immediately fell into his hustle. Shooting dice was his thing. He was good at it and soon everyone came to know it. Ernest would walk into a dice game with nothing and leave with over $100, which was a lot of money in 1960.

Ernest met Anna Marie – or "Slim" as he called her – the same night Sharon met Adam. And just like my parents, Ernest and Slim would deal with one another off and on pretty much the rest of their lives. Still, that spirit of restlessness ran deep within Ernest.

One night, Ernest asked his brother Donald to drop him off in Hunt's Point, in the Bronx. It was 1968; there was nothing but trouble in Hunt's Point, but Ernest assured his brother he knew what he was doing. Ernest came home hours later with hundreds of dollars and a car, the deed signed over by a man who couldn't shoot dice nearly as well as Ernest.

"Check this out," Ernest said, stretching his arm out and pointing to a small red puncture on the inside of his elbow. "What's that?" Donald asked. When the loser ran out of money, he'd paid Ernest in heroin.

Donald made Ernest promise not to try heroin again: "That's some bad, bad stuff and you don't want to be mixed up in that." Ernest gave his word, and being a man of his word was good enough for his brother.

Donald, who was fresh out of the service, moved to Oakland, California. Nearly a decade would pass before Ernest admitted to his brother that he'd been using heroin long before that night in Hunt's Point.

I don't remember actually meeting Ernest Prince. He was always on the outskirts of my life. I knew him as Anna Marie's boyfriend. One day, when I was nine years old and Zenia was ten, Ernest picked us up and took us fishing. My mother and his grandmother, MoMo, came along. We spent the entire day out at the lake. I remember MoMo catching fish after fish to the point where I went over to her side because I couldn't catch even a nibble. She just laughed as she watched me. I still couldn't catch a thing. But I remember her smile being enough. She felt warm. That entire day felt warm. It didn't feel strange to me at all.

I didn't see MoMo again until the day Anna Marie walked my mother and I into the Prince family reunion some six years later. She was just as warm. Only now, it felt strange.

After the family reunion, I changed. Like I said, I felt like a part of me had died. I loved Adam Hackett, and I loved his wife Pat. You see, Adam and Pat met years before I was born. Pat was a good girl from a good family, and Adam told her right away he was going to marry her. Eventually, he kept his word and proposed. Of course she said yes, but a few months into the engagement, Adam confessed to Pat that he had a two-year-old son. Pat was devastated, but she was also in love, so she asked to meet me.

It was love at first sight. Even to this day, Pat exudes a warmth and kindness that draws everyone in. Even my mother, who'd been dating Adam without knowing he was engaged, couldn't dislike Pat. Pat loved me since the first time she saw me, but she had heard the rumblings that Adam may not be my father. She'd asked my mother, "Is this boy Adam's? Because I'm going to marry Adam Hackett and I plan to love this little boy like my own." My mother told her yes, and that was all Pat needed to hear.

Pat took me everywhere. She made running errands and trips to the grocery store feel like an adventure. I loved her and my daddy, and after the family reunion, I was afraid I would lose them both. Once Adam found out about Ernest, there would be no more running errands with Pat. My entire world would change. I began to mourn, a feeling which would stick with me for years to come. I felt like I was losing my daddy. I wanted to talk to Pat, but I couldn't. I couldn't talk to anyone, so I mourned alone.

Over time, I started going over to the Prince house. Adam and I weren't getting along. I was in the streets more than I was in school, and he didn't respect hustling. So we were keeping our distance from one another. Still, even though I didn't tell my mom or Pat, I liked visiting the Prince house. I liked being around MoMo, Ernest's grandmother Nano, and all of his brothers. It felt right in ways I didn't even know how to explain. For one thing, Ernest and I were a lot alike. Aside from the fact that I looked just like him, we were both hustlers who never took our mind off a dollar. We both loved the streets, and had an intuition which saved both of our lives on more than one occasion.

I don't recall there ever being a formal conversation about Ernest Prince being my father. No one ever sat me down and explained anything to me. Eventually, Adam caught wind of the amount of time I was spending with Ernest, and that was a problem. As far as he, my mother and Pat were concerned, Adam Hackett was my one and only father. They didn't care how much circumstantial evidence I presented. In their eyes I was Adam's boy, end of story.

I look back on it now with a sense of irony. All the years I spent in mourning, thinking that accepting Ernest Prince would mean losing Adam Hackett, couldn't have been farther from the truth. As I'm writing this book, I've realized how valuable both Adam and Ernest were in my life.

If it hadn't been for the discipline and structure Adam instilled in me, and the lessons he taught me about respect, I couldn't be the man that

I am today. I'm forever grateful to him for the unconditional love he shared with me.

I'm thankful to Ernest for bringing me into this world, and for all the wisdom he shared with me along the way. He gave me confidence and helped me realize that I was wiser than I even knew. Most of all, I can't even begin to explain how much meeting the relatives on the Prince side of my family filled a void in my life. I was able to spend time with my 114-year-old great-grandmother MoMo, who shared a lot of wisdom with me, and also Ernest's mother Nano, and so many other uncles and cousins – too many to name.

I would advise anyone who is living without meeting their mother or father to find them. Number one, you don't wanna cross the bloodlines and end up dating one of your family members because you didn't know any better. Number two, where your health is concerned, it's such an advantage to be able to observe the genetics of those who have gone before you.

It wasn't until I was 22 years old that Adam and Ernest made their peace. It was around the time I opened a car lot. I'd always had a passion for cars, and I was dating a girl who's father was a car salesman and helped me get a dealer's license. I learned the rules of the car business quickly and became the most profitable dealership among twenty or so dealerships on Shepherd Street - I knew because all of us used the same accountant.

Ernest and his brother Larry often came by the car lot to hang out. One day, Adam showed up. He was agitated, and you could see a pistol sticking out of his waistband of his pants. In Texas in the late 1980s, carrying a gun was common, especially for Adam. But on this day, he wanted Ernest to know he had a strap. He asked to speak with him outside. From what we could hear, Adam told Ernest to stay away from me. He said that I was his son, and he didn't want Ernest hanging around.

Ernest told Adam he couldn't do that. He respected Adam, but that was asking too much. "He's my son, Adam," was the last thing we heard Ernest say before the two former best friends moved out of earshot. Larry and I watched from inside as they talked for fifteen more minutes. Finally, they reached some sort of peace, and they embraced.

We didn't know it at the time, but Adam was sick. He'd smoked two packs of menthol cigarettes a day throughout my entire life, and lung cancer was eating him alive. When Adam died a few months later, I was right there to comfort Pat and make sure my father had a proper burial.

But I was a Prince all along and didn't even know it.

Looking back, I'm thankful for both of my fathers, who have since left this planet and crossed over to heaven.

LEADERS, FOLLOWERS, & LONERS

I'm a natural-born leader. There's something in me that needs to be the head, the top dog, the man in charge. I learned this about myself very early on, in the same place that most of us first learn about ourselves: school.

My desire to dominate began in kindergarten. I was enrolled in Dogan Elementary School, a co-ed school on the north side of Fifth Ward. Every year I'd spend the first few days of school observing my classroom, learning the lay of the land, and most importantly, learning the weak spots of each of my classmates. You see, everyone has something. There isn't a person on God's green earth who doesn't have some vulnerability that – if they're not careful – can be used against them. And I was into finding them and using them to my benefit. At that age, most kids' vulnerability stemmed from wanting to belong, to be liked. There really are only three types of people in this world: leaders, followers, and loners.

The vulnerability of a leader is often their own ego, which makes them unable to submit. Everyone, at some point in life, must learn to submit when necessary. In the streets, you may have to submit to a supplier who switches up the terms, or a police officer who's riding you pretty tough. At home you may have to submit to your spouse to keep the peace. In business, submission can be a great short-term tactic towards a long-term goal. But if your ego won't allow you to submit when necessary, it becomes a liability.

Luckily for me, I learned to submit to God above all else. You can't become a great leader without being a great follower. That relationship taught me the ultimate humility and made me feel as though I never needed to submit to man.

It's easy to identify the vulnerability in a follower: they want to belong. Most people crave safety in numbers. The best parallel is a shepherd and his flock. One shepherd can herd hundreds of sheep at a time, but with that power comes great responsibility. Day in and day out, it's his job to make sure the sheep have food, water, and are kept safe. The job of the sheep is simple: follow. But sheep fail to understand that they both share the risk. While the shepherd bets on the outside world, weathering elements, using instincts to find food or avoid potential danger, the sheep take the biggest risk by betting everything – their very lives – on one man. The followers who understand this actually hold more power than the shepherd. They use their consent to follow as their currency. These informed followers are few and far between. But it's the blind followers, those who don't realize the power they possess just by staying within the herd, who are the most vulnerable. And also the most useful. Once you've earned their trust, they'll follow you anywhere. And gaining their trust is simple: you assert yourself as the shepherd. Followers are governed by their fear.

The Fifth Ward taught me how to fight. I spent a lot of time hanging out with the older guys on the block who had seven or eight years on me, and they made sure I knew how to throw hands when necessary. They'd shadowbox with me, teaching me maneuvers which many kids my age didn't know. I was smaller than most kids my age, but the older guys taught me how use that as an advantage. Being smaller meant I could move faster. I required less energy to move, so I had more energy to use. These lessons on the streets gave me a strategy to take into the classroom.

Once I determined the leaders, followers, and loners, I'd make my move to dominate. You don't need to strike every sheep to instill fear. You only need to hit one. The right one. Picking on a weak sheep will only make you a weak shepherd, and that's not what you want. So my strategy was to identify a weaker leader or even an informed follower and get them to submit.

Anyone with eyes could see how small I was, so the fact that I was willing to challenge my classmates already let them know what kind of person I was: aggressive and unafraid to take risks. It helped that I knew how to fight, too, and wasn't afraid to follow through on my threats. I'd meet classmates in the bathrooms and intimidate them when necessary. Sometimes it would escalate into an actual fight. But fighting in school was difficult. Back then we didn't get suspended, we got paddled. So I began challenging kids to fight after school. Word would spread that a challenge had been laid down, and everyone would make a plan to go watch. It became a spectacle. By 3 PM there would be a crowd waiting, cheering, ready to see who my latest victim would be… if they showed up at all. Many kids didn't accept the challenge. The challenge alone was enough to make them submit. But for the rest of them — call it pride, resilience or outright gumption — all it would take was one fight and my reign was renewed as the top dog.

But I didn't win them all. By second grade, my reputation preceded me. When I challenged Big Carl to fight in the bathroom, all the boys in our class came to watch. Big Carl was twice my size, but I was determined to get the best of him. I had him for a while; I was whooping Big Carl good. He'd been giving me trouble in class, and no one thought I would challenge him simply because he was Big Carl; he had a reputation of his own. But that only meant I had to challenge him, for several reasons.

First, even the most popular king must remind everyone of their own mortality. If you reign too long and soar too high for extended periods of time, people can't identify with you and their respect becomes resentment.

But the most important reason I had to challenge Big Carl was because there was a chance I might actually lose. An easy fight is just "sparring," a boxing term for a practice fight where you're just going through the motions. No one's landing any heavy punches because it's just a training exercise. Sparring is a great way to stay in shape, but to actually learn how to box, you need the pressure of a real fight.

At first Big Carl was taking his licks; I was slipping out of his grasp, running circles around him. I was using all my advantages to the fullest. And then he caught me with a clean punch in my face. I felt like his fist had moved my nose from one side of my face to the other. Blood came pouring from my nose. I flung my head back, trying to stop the bleeding.

The fight ended with Big Carl's knockout punch, but I didn't consider it a loss. I'd challenged Big Carl because no one challenged Big Carl; I knew there was a good possibility that I might lose. But I gave it my all. So even when his devastating blow came, I'd already made my point.

People follow the convicted. Someone who believes in something so much that they are willing to die for it will always be more appealing than someone who's not willing to take the risk. It's classic David versus Goliath. Even when the odds are against you, the fact that you're still willing to fight is sometimes enough to earn respect. I don't pick easy fights. Losing a title fight will always matter more than winning a spar.

I gained a two-part lesson from my fight with Big Carl: Don't get hit, and don't ever fear a man. Once I established dominance over my classmates, the real work began. Just like a shepherd, I had to provide for my flock. Remember, the sheep follow because they're benefitting from you. You can't lead if you don't have anything to offer.

I always had several hustles, whether it was my lawn-mowing business or selling eggs from my chicken coup. I've always had more than one way to make a dollar. But all of those hustles required manpower. And what better workforce than the flock you already lead?

I believe that everyone should eat. It is my job as a shepherd to make sure that my flock is well tended and cared for, for without them, I cannot eat. Again, it's that mutual trust and respect. We all take risks on each other, so the victories belong to everyone willing to work. Leadership isn't only about dominating; it's about providing.

Let me be clear, there's nothing wrong with being a follower. Everyone can't lead. And to be a great leader, you have to know how to follow. But a shepherd without a flock isn't a shepherd. He's just a wandering man with a stick.

BREAKING THE POVERTY CURSE

THE ART & SCIENCE OF
respect

My relationship with money started early. Most children have chores around the house, and if you're lucky and your family can afford it, you get an allowance. My mother worked as a waitress and would bring her tip money home, where I waited. I enjoyed counting up the coins and adding them to my bankroll. I was a great saver. I knew the value of having something put away. The money was power; it represented options. And where I'm from, the more options the better.

I sold marijuana when I was eleven years old, which isn't uncommon for young impoverished children. But my introduction to the drug trade was nothing like the overdramatic boys on the corner you'd see on television shows like *The Wire*. Their lives were not like mine.

One of the biggest dangers in urban areas is proximity. Desperation can only touch those in its immediate vicinity. If your neighbor is desperate and willing to do anything to feed himself and his family, he's more of a threat to you if he's in the apartment across the hall. Where else can he go? An impoverished person doesn't usually have many options. He may set up shop in the stairwell you have to walk through every single day, and eventually he's going to need help. He might even recruit your children to work for him, and why wouldn't they? Your kids have seen him every day of their lives in the courtyard, in the laundry room, saying hello to you as you pick up your mail. He's your neighbor. It's only a matter of time before his desperation becomes yours.

Rich people often wonder why poor people destroy their own neighborhoods. The answer? Because they can't get to yours. Proximity.

If Houston has an abundance of anything, it's land, and space means opportunity. In many ways, the desperation in the country is a quieter epidemic. There's a tension that comes with living so close to other people in urban areas. Seeing the same people every day breeds contempt. When your stomach is growling, you start to take mental notes of your neighbor's situation. *What kind of clothes are they wearing? Was there a Christmas tree in the window this year? How'd they get the car fixed and running again?* And eventually you start asking yourself, *What do they have and how can I get it?*

The space in rural areas alleviates that tension. Your neighbor might only be in the next row house but even that extra thirty feet – having your own walkway – is enough to eliminate those questions.

One of the boys I went to school with was named James Ryan. I considered him a follower. He was tall and slow, but had no idea of his own strength, which made him easy to dominate. We were both in the third grade, into sports, chasing little girls and goofing off when the bell let out. Some afternoons I'd go over to his house and we'd play and be normal kids, looking for trouble to get into until his father came home from work.

I was already deep into my own entrepreneurial ventures by then. My mowing business was steady, I fixed mini-bike engines and sold eggs. Within the city of Houston, it's illegal to have chickens, so I'd already had to move my operation a few times, from my auntie's house to my grandmother's house. I sold eggs for a dollar a dozen. People liked buying eggs from me because they were fresh; they'd still be warm sometimes. Some of my biggest customers were my neighbors.

All the money I made back then, I'd spend it on mini-bikes. A mini-bike is kinda like a go-kart or a motorcycle. It has a motor in it, but it's not as powerful as a dirt bike. I'd learned how to build them from fixing lawnmowers, because they used the same type of Briggs & Stratton engine. After my bicycle was stolen, I took a motor from a lawnmowing edger, added a clutch, and had a mini-bike. That's how I ended up with another side hustle, fixing mini-bike engines.

Even while I was playing, I was always looking for opportunities to make money. That opportunity came through James Ryan, and he didn't even know it.

Growing up in the hood meant you were exposed to all sorts of different hustles. Some of the same guys who taught me how to fight taught me how to gamble, shoot dice and craps. And one day, I overheard them talking about selling marijuana. I knew from a young age that being a corner boy wasn't for me. I didn't want to work for someone who was working for someone else, both of us making only pennies. But it was a pretty simple business model. The guy on the corner sold what the big boss bagged up. But the product in the bag had to come from somewhere, and I knew where to get it: James Ryan's house.

James' father kept a garden behind his house, which was full of tomatoes, collard greens, and cucumbers. But growing alongside the family's vegetables were rows and rows of marijuana. So late one night, I brought a friend with me over to James' house and climbed into the backyard. We pulled three or four plants out of the ground and ran straight to the hustlers on the corner. I'd hit a jackpot. He gave me ten dollars per plant, and told me there was plenty more where that came from if I could get my hands on more. And I could. At least once or twice a week I'd call down to James' house making small talk just so I could find out who was home.

The biggest threat to my operation was James' father. He was growing so many that he wouldn't miss one or two a week, but if he caught us in the act, I was sure there'd be consequences. Somehow, we pulled it off two or three more times. A quick trip would earn $20 - $30. That doesn't sound like a lot of money now. These days, kids spend that much weekly on iTunes. But in 1974, $20 was enough to buy groceries for the entire household. And I was making it in a few minutes.

I still remember the day my Aunt Teddy's lights were cut off. We were living in an apartment in Third Ward at the time, right above hers. She was talking with my mother in our living room, with tears in her eyes, at a loss for what to do. When everyone around you is as strapped as you are, it's hard to keep the faith and hope that things will get better. But my Aunt Teddy did. While my sister and cousins played, I listened to their conversation. Teddy noticed me watching and declared to my mother that I was a "peculiar" child.

"God loves us all, but He has His chosen ones," she said. It would be years before I understood what the word "peculiar" meant, but I knew what it meant to be "chosen." Without a word I went to my bedroom and returned with $19 to get Aunt Teddy's lights turned back on.

That night introduced me to the idea that God had plans for me. Aunt Teddy's words planted a seed in me. Handing her the money I'd saved up from my various hustles gave me a high. I felt like I was contributing to something, and it's the ability to contribute which separates those who are actually living from those who are merely alive. I don't believe in being passive with your life, even your struggle. Your circumstances don't have to be the end of your story.

My desire to contribute transformed my impoverished life. I couldn't live every day watching my loved ones suffer. They were a part of me. Their tears were my tears. They couldn't see a path out of the bondage of poverty, but I could. And I knew I would have to lead them.

I never told James about my hustle. When you're on a mission, focused on your money, you have to be willing to make the hard decisions. Every friend can't be a business partner. Plus, James had already disqualified himself. Those plants had been growing in his yard long before I came along, and James walked past those same hustlers every day like I did. But it had never occurred to him to put a deal together. You don't get paid just for being there.

Truth is, I didn't trust that James wouldn't give me up. And even though we were friends, I wasn't friends with his dad. I didn't like him; he didn't like us. He was a mean, bad person; those ass-whoopins he used to give James would be considered child abuse today. In my eyes, he deserved to get got. And that's how I became a marijuana wholesaler at eleven years old.

CONSPIRACY

(kuhn-spir-uh-see)- noun:
An agreement by two or more persons to commit a crime, fraud, or other wrongful act.

When my friend Frank ran away from home at eleven years old, my grandmother let him come stay with us. Although we didn't have much, my grandmother believed that no one, especially a child, should go without. By then, I had several viable hustles going. My lawnmowing business was growing by leaps and bounds. At five dollars per yard, I was able to outsource most of the work to my friends, making sure they got a cut of the take-home pay. My neighbors, Mr. Rudy and Mr. Brown, had taught me how to fix engines, so I handled the lawnmower maintenance myself. My family always encouraged my work ethic, so I started a side job on the weekends working with a welder, Henry Martin, who was dating my mother.

Frank had helped with one of my early entrepreneurial ventures. When I was about nine years old, Frank and I went hunting near my older cousin's house. We came across this horse, a Shetland pony, and I thought it was lost. I didn't realize that we were on somebody's property, so I kinda felt like the horse was a free horse. Me and Frank ran this horse down and we finally caught him three or four miles away. We walked the horse back to my cousin's.

My objective was to bring the pony home and make money off it the same way I'd seen the carnival making money off ponies. So I called my mother and she put my stepfather Henry Martin on the phone. I told him I wanted to bring the horse home. He told me, "Boy, you ain't found no horse, leave that horse where you discovered him."

I didn't listen to him. I convinced my cousin to help me load the horse into the back of his van and gave him like $7 for gas to drive the horse back to the Fifth Ward. So I brought this horse to the city and I was charging 25 cents for pony rides. I'd just put people on the horse and walk him around the house. I made a few dollars and I had a little line of kids waiting, but it wasn't long before my stepfather's green welding truck pulled up. He put a real good whipping on me that night with his bare hands. That was my first and only whupping he gave me.

Anyway, if Frank was going to live with us, he'd have to work, too. But unlike my other friends, Frank had already identified his talent. Frank was a natural-born thief. He loved to steal. He couldn't help himself. It didn't matter what it was, he just loved the thrill of stealing, and he was unhappy when he didn't have the opportunity to steal.

For me, this posed a challenge. I wasn't big on stealing. I wasn't afraid to roll my sleeves up and get down to hard work. But I did have a problem with passing up an opportunity, and Frank was an opportunity.

Every morning my grandmother would see Frank and I off to school, but Frank would never make it to class. As much as he loved stealing, he hated school. So he'd skip it. Frank is a follower, and his vulnerability rang true: he wanted my acceptance. That's the obvious reason he came to live with me after running away from his own family. He wanted to make me happy, and I wanted to put Frank to good use. So every morning, since Frank was going to skip school anyway, I gave him an assignment. His challenge every day was to steal something different: maybe some chickens, or an edger with a motor on it for my mini-bikes. No assignment was too big or too small; Frank never shied away from the challenge. He lived for it. Frank was a kleptomaniac.

As a leader, I was recognizing Frank's passion and using it to benefit everyone. This went on for a few years. The assignments got more challenging and Frank got better at completing them. My grandmother had no idea that Frank was my own personal booster. Looking back on it now, it was incredible the things he was able to steal. This was truly his gift and his curse.

We were in the eighth grade when the curse kicked in. On this particular morning Frank's assignment was to get a rooster that I wanted. Back then, in 1977, we had rooster fights. It was a very physically aggressive time. Now, I just collect roosters. They're beautiful creatures that I enjoy watching and listening to as they crow in the background. But back then there was one rooster in particular I'd seen and I knew he needed to be my fighter.

A few hours later I was in class when Principal Ross summoned me to his office. Frank had been boosting for us for years and had never gotten caught, so he was the last thing on my mind as I walked down the hall. Principal Ross' reputation was hard earned. Although he was only the assistant principal, everyone knew that he didn't play. "Son, you know Frank?" he asked as I walked into his office. I told him yes.

"Well Frank didn't make it to school today," he said, to which I replied, "Well, I'm here. I've been here all day." But that wasn't his point.

"Your grandmother says that you got Frank skipping school," Principal Ross said.

My heart skipped a beat when I realized my grandmother was giving me up. You see, while I feared no man, I definitely feared my grandmother. And now I knew that she knew something was up.

"My grandmother?" I asked.

"Yes, she wants to speak with you," he said, as he handed me the phone. I wouldn't call the exchange between my grandmother and I a "conversation." She'd been told from someone else that it was my fault Frank was skipping school. And I was starting to understand what had happened. The truancy officer had picked up Frank.

It wasn't the stealing that got him in trouble; it was what he was neglecting while doing his dirt. Like many other criminals, Frank had overlooked one important fact: it's not the extra that draws attention. It's the failure to maintain the normal that usually gets you caught.

Principal Ross took the phone from me and assured my grandmother he'd handle it. You see, Principal Ross had no idea Frank was stealing for me. In his eyes, the big offense here was that Frank was not in class every day. As far as he and my grandmother were concerned, this was my fault. Everyone knew that if I told Frank to jump, his response would be, "How high?"

"Do you know what 'conspiracy' means, son?" Mr. Ross asked me as he stood up and came around his desk.

I'd heard the word before, but I didn't know what it meant.

Today, anyone who's ever dealt with the law knows what the word *conspiracy* means, because it's at the center of the RICO law. In 1970, Congress passed the Racketeer Influenced and Corrupt Organizations (RICO) Act, which was aimed at the Mafia. It was an effort to establish severe consequences for people who belong to criminal organizations which are responsible for crimes such as murder, kidnapping, extortion, witness tampering, robbery, arson, or even financial crimes such as money laundering, wire fraud, and counterfeiting. Eventually, the RICO law grew as a way of targeting drug crimes. The RICO law allows the federal government to prosecute someone for simply knowing of a crime or being in the presence of a crime, even if they didn't commit it themselves. It's a federal bully tactic which has brought down just as many innocent people as guilty.

Decades after my meeting with Mr. Ross, as I went to war against the United States government to fight this very accusation of being a *conspirator*, I'd think back to that day Frank got caught skipping class. Being a leader isn't only about providing for your flock. There's a responsibility that comes with having a following. That's why it's important to pick the right following. Because if a sheep does the wrong thing, as the shepherd, you too will be punished.

As Mr. Ross rounded his desk, he picked up his paddle and explained that "conspiracy" meant that while I didn't actually commit the offense, I was guilty by association. It didn't matter that I had an excellent attendance record or that I was getting good grades. That was expected of me. But it was also expected of Frank, who was under my influence. So at that point, I had to pay the price for getting caught up in a conspiracy. That price was Mr. Ross spelling "CONSPIRACY" on my ass with that paddle, and I never forgot it.

Heavy is the head that wears the crown.

COMING OF AGE

THE ART & SCIENCE OF
respect

In tenth grade I left my stepfather Henry Martin's house and moved in with my father, Adam Hackett, and his wife Pat. Aside from the third grade, when I spent a year living with my mother in the Third Ward, I'd never lived outside of Fifth Ward. I'd never lived in a middle-class brick home. But both my mother and father felt I needed a change of environment, so there I was in Kashmere Gardens, an upwardly mobile suburb of Houston. Aside from being away from the roaches and rats, trash and other signs of poverty that had become normal, the real shock to my system was the structure my father imposed on me as soon as I arrived.

Until then, most of my discipline had been self-imposed. Although it was impressive for a fifteen-year-old, it was nothing like what my father had in store for me. His father, Irvin Hackett, was known for being stern. He demanded respect and total control of his household. He was such a disciplinarian that Adam moved out of his father's house at 17, opting to finish high school while living on his own. The irony, of course, is that Adam's apple didn't fall far from the tree.

Right away, I had a problem with being forced to use the word "Sir." This was 1979, a time of black power and rebellion, and I was 15. To me, "Yes sir" and "No sir" was some slavemaster shit, but to my father, it was non-negotiable. I had to adjust or get out. The other dealbreaker was that I had to finish high school. Only a few people in my family had a high school diploma, and it was incredibly important to my mother that I complete school. My mother had dropped out due to the strain of three pregnancies, two small children and a stillborn, so it was her dream to see me break the cycle.

I wanted to quit school after the ninth grade. I felt like I'd learned enough to get out into the workforce and earn some good money. I considered becoming a welder. I'd been training under my stepfather, Henry Martin, and it was a trade that paid him $25 an hour, good money in those days. But my father had another idea.

In my father's house, there was structure, and I had responsibilities. I went to school every day, made my bed, cleaned up after myself, did my homework, and when I wasn't doing those things, I was working with him. I woke up every morning at 5 AM to start my father's car so it would warm up, and in the winter, I had to scrape all the ice off the windshield in time for him to leave for work.

At night and on the weekends, I worked on cars with my father. Head jobs were the worst; we had to take apart entire engines to get it out of the car and repair or replace it. It was heavy labor. And the most appalling thing of all was the fact that I wasn't getting paid. According to my father, my compensation was the fact that I was able to live under his roof, eat his food he provided, and wear the clothes he provided. All of my side hustles had to go.

I was miserable at the time, but looking back on it now, it was the best thing for me. Adam was showing me how to be a man. I already knew how to be a hustler; I even knew how to be a boss. But thanks to my father, I was learning how to be the head of a household. Respect was a big deal to me; it still is. But until that point, I knew more about getting respect than giving it. My father was teaching me the proper way to give respect, and I was fighting it tooth and nail.

Adam Hackett made it very plain: it was his way or the highway. I got kicked out several times, but the last time was enough to change my mind.

I don't even recall why Adam had put me out, but I'm sure it had to do with me not following one of his many rules. I'd gone back to the Fifth Ward. I was happy to be home, back in a world where I was in control. I had my crew again; I had time for girls, time to hang out. It was just like old times, as if nothing had changed.

But one thing *had* changed. My crew had been robbing the local McDonald's. They hit other restaurants just outside the neighborhood six or seven times, too. After every score they'd come to school the next day with big bankrolls of cash. At first I wanted no parts of it. I just knew they were going to get caught. But I kept seeing the new cash, the new shoes, the jewelry, and eventually gave in. I knew it was a huge risk, so I decided I would be the driver. I figured I could make the same amount of cash without having to go in the store or point a pistol.

When I picked them up, they were wearing long trenchcoats to hide their weapons. They'd hit this McDonald's twice before already, so they thought they knew the weak spots. After I dropped them off, I noticed a police car waiting across the street under the underpass. I guess the police figured that if my friends were stupid enough to rob the same McDonald's twice, they'd be stupid enough to hit it three times.

The police were right. I blew the horn, signaling for my friends to come back. They got back into the car without going inside the McDonald's, but that was close enough for me. My short-lived career as a getaway driver was over. I accepted it as a warning.

I dropped my homies off and we went our separate ways. I drove home, thinking about how close I'd come to getting arrested. I saw it as a sign from God. That wasn't the life I wanted for myself. Being incarcerated wouldn't get my mother her house, or me my land, and it sure wouldn't break the cycle of poverty that had such a firm hold on my family. I started thinking about going back to my father's house. Maybe his rules, however strict, were there to make me better.

That night marked the first significant time in my life when I instinctively acted on a warning sign that kept me from tragedy. The second time, years later, also involved a McDonald's - but we'll get to that later.

The next morning, I awoke to the news. After I'd dropped my friends off, they decided to hit a different McDonald's. I didn't know Marvin very well, but apparently he was the weak link. They were all in jail for armed robbery, charged as adults, and eventually served 8-10 years in prison. Most of them never got the opportunity to graduate high school.

So I went back to my father's house. But this time, Pat, my stepmother, convinced him to let me get a job. For the next few months, when I wasn't in school, I was bagging groceries at Food City grocery store. But it wasn't long before trouble found me.

Occasionally, there'd be a customer who couldn't pay for their groceries. They'd already done all their shopping and realized at the cash register that they'd forgotten their money or checkbook. When that happened, we'd set the groceries to the side and give them a chance to come back. If they didn't return, we'd restock the groceries on the shelves.

It was the 4th of July holiday weekend and the store was packed with people preparing for their barbecues. I had a Mexican friend who bagged groceries in the next aisle. He and I weren't particularly close; we'd never hung out outside of work. But we were cool enough to pass the time keeping each other entertained. On this particular day he'd bagged an entire cart full of groceries, and the family had to go home and get their money. But this cart, full of meat and other premium goods, was just sitting there. Finally, my Mexican friend came to me and said, "Let me put this in your car and we'll split the groceries when we get off."

This was 1983, and I was driving a 1950 Chevy. I liked my old car. I'd chosen it on purpose. I liked that it was different from what everyone else was driving. It stood out, and I stood out in it. It also had a large trunk. After thinking about it for a few minutes, I figured, *Why not? What's the worst that could happen?* I gave him the keys and he took the abandoned cart out to my car and put all the groceries into my trunk and we both went back to work.

A while later, the family returned for their food. I said nothing. But it only took a few minutes for the Mexican guy to tell them that I'd taken the groceries. The police were called. When the officer asked for the keys to my car, I knew it was a wrap. It didn't matter that I wasn't the one who came up with the idea or who put the food in my car. It was in my car and my Mexican "friend" said I did it, so I was promptly fired, arrested, and taken to the police station.

I spent the entire ride in the back of the police car thinking about my father. I knew it was over. He'd taken me back after my short-lived return to the Fifth Ward, and truthfully, I didn't want to go back there again. I didn't want to disappoint him, either; I was afraid he'd give up on me. So I called my stepmother Pat instead.

Pat had been advocating for me since the first day she met me, when I was only two years old. She said she loved me instantly, and she'd spent my entire life showing me how much at every chance she got. She'd lobbied on my behalf so I could get a paying job instead of working for free at my father's mechanic shop. And here I was in the police station, accused of stealing a cart of groceries from the job she'd helped me get. I was ashamed, and scared of what would happen when I got home.

When Pat arrived at the police station to get me out, she told me, "Look, I'll make a deal with you. If you give me your word that you will never steal again, I won't tell your daddy about what happened here today." I felt like an angel had come down from above and I'd been given another chance.

I gave her my word, and I meant it. For years to come, I'd have the opportunity to take things that didn't belong to me. But I'd remember that I'd given my word to Pat, who never wanted to do anything but be on my side. Giving her my word made me do the right thing. I wanted to do right by Pat and I wanted to do right by myself, because I couldn't go to jail. My life was about to change.

Living in Kashmere Gardens was the first time in my life that I was a loner. I'd met a few people but I hadn't grown up with them, so I would never call them real friends. Kashmere was so different from the Fifth Ward. I grew up in the hood. I knew grimy. I understood our lingo. I was used to dealing day in and day out with the dealers and the thugs. But now I was in the middle class. Everyone was clean cut; preppy, even. I spoke less and observed more. My three years in Kashmere Gardens felt like going off to college. It was an opportunity to live outside of my native environment and redirect my focus. With the absence of my crew, I concentrated on earning money. I'd been working my entire life but this was the first time that I wasn't working with a family member or for myself. Now I was learning what it's like to be an employee.

I love the Fifth Ward. It's a special place that will always be a part of me. But I know that if I stayed there, instead of moving to Kashmere

Gardens with my father, there's a strong possibility that I would've ended up a statistic like so many of my friends. I needed that separation from the hood to gain perspective. Eventually I was able to return to help the hood, but first I needed to help myself. I didn't like having to ask anyone for money, so I'd come to rely on my own income to meet my needs. And my needs were rapidly expanding.

BLESSING IN DISGUISE

My junior year of high school, I enrolled in a typing class, which I hated. First of all, there was no way I wanted to sit in front of a typewriter. It felt like something a secretary would do, and that wasn't me. But my real problem – the truth behind my objection to the class – was that the teacher was gay. Mr. Arnold was openly gay at a time when I didn't know any other gay men.

It was 1982, and sodomy was illegal in the state of Texas. In the hood, it was enough to get you beat up. I'd grown up disliking homosexuals. It's not something I'm proud of, but at the time, right or wrong, that's how I felt. Where I'm from, you had to be tough in order to survive. A man with feminine mannerisms was seen as weak, and we ate weakness alive. I couldn't understand why a man would choose to be with another man. It sounded and looked wrong, unnatural and against the laws of nature.

Years later I realized that I had no business judging anyone for their lifestyle or who they were as a person. And while homosexuality still seems unnatural and wrong to me, I'm mature enough now to understand that everyone is different and I don't have the right to judge anyone. This was a lesson that took me several years to truly learn. But it began with me learning to type.

At the time, I hated Mr. Arnold for being gay, and I hated the idea of being in his class. I tried everything to get out of that class. I even had Pat talk to the principal on my behalf. But no matter how hard I tried, I was stuck, so I decided to just wait it out. I just sat in class, refusing to participate, and for three weeks, Mr. Arnold said nothing. Finally, as I was leaving one day, he said, "You know you're failing, don't you?"

I'd never failed a class before. I'd gotten D's, but in my entire academic history, I'd never gotten an F, and I wasn't about to start now. My desire to succeed was greater than my hate for this man. So I began to try, and lo and behold, I turned out to be an excellent typist. In fact, I became one of the best in the class.

Over time, Mr. Arnold began encouraging me, teaching me ways that I could become better. I started to see him not as a gay man, but simply as a human being, someone who just wanted to help me. And his help was working. I ended up with an A in his class and could type over 60 words per minute.

When I returned to school my senior year, I was invited to join OEA (Office Educational Association), a work-study program for high school students with exceptional office skills. I was one of only three students chosen from the school, and it was because of my typing! If

I'd succeeded in getting out of the class, it would've confirmed my belief that I didn't need to learn how to type, and it would've reinforced my homophobia. Staying in class challenged me to think outside my narrow views and also learn a new skill, which expanded my world even further.

While participating in the program, half of my school day was spent in class, and the other half was spent working in a real office. Two of the jobs were with Exxon Oil, but I chose the third position, working as a Teller's Assistant at Colonial Savings & Loan Bank. My duties were simple enough. I spent most of my time filing paperwork and helping the tellers with whatever they needed. In the meantime, I'd finished school and made my mother proud by receiving my high school diploma. But I was still focused on my promise to myself: I hadn't yet bought her a house.

All the bank employees liked me. At the end of each day I'd help them count all the money, which was my favorite part. I'd never seen so much cash in one place. Every day I felt the temptation. *I could just take a little bit home, flip it, and bring it back in the morning,* I thought on more than one occasion. But then I'd remember my conversation with Pat, and I knew I couldn't steal that money. I had given my stepmother my word.

One day, I spotted some counterfeit bills a customer was trying to pass through the window. That earned me a promotion to the main office. Now I was a Loan Vault Custodian, keeping track of all the loan files and assisting the officers with customer applications. I felt like I was on the right track. Everyone was pleased with the work I was doing. I even convinced them to hire my girlfriend as a teller. Money was important then, because she was pregnant with my first child.

I still had bigger dreams, so I sought out the bank president, who I'd learned was the highest paid employee. His car was dirty, so I offered to clean it for him. It was a strategic move to establish some kind of business relationship with him; the best way to get a piece of someone's time is to earn it. Once I had his attention, I had a million questions about how to become the president of the bank. He told me that I should go to college, study finance, and put in time at a branch. I thought maybe this was my way; this was how I would build my fortune.

Shortly after that conversation, I was called into a meeting and told that the entire department was being laid off. And just like that, my time at the bank was over. I was devastated. I'd been plotting to become president of a bank and build my fortune, and now I was out of a job with a baby on the way. It was a wake-up call. The truth is, working for someone, putting in your time and building equity within a company is commendable. But if you don't own it, you have no control over how much time you have.

I left the bank that day with a fire in the pit of my stomach. It was a life-changing moment. I decided right then and there that I would never work for someone else again. I remember sitting in my mother's kitchen that night, hurt and disappointed, venting. "So this is how they do you, huh, ma? They build your hopes up and then just cut you loose?" I was angry. "I ain't working for nobody else!"

"Boy, hush," she told me. "Go find another job. Don't act like that." My mother had put in time at countless jobs throughout my childhood. I can't tell you how many mornings I watched her go off to work, still tired from the day before, only to come home to take care of us, get a few hours of sleep and do it all over again. My mother had been a waitress, a store clerk, and everything in between, but she was still broke. It didn't make sense to me. The idea of exchanging your life for minimum wage, only to have it taken away from you at any moment, was absurd. It was slavery. And I wasn't going to do it.

I've never been afraid of hard work. I spent half of my childhood working myself to exhaustion, and the only time it bothered me was when I was working for someone else. The feeling of not being in control of my own destiny was something I never wanted to feel again. I'd never been the type of person who was content with taking orders. Even though my time working at the grocery store and the bank was short, I learned many skills through those experiences. But the most unforgettable lesson I gained from corporate America came to me as I was packing my things on my last day at the bank: always bet on myself.

My mother was still living in poverty, my girlfriend was seven months pregnant, and I needed to do something fast. So I went back to the place where I first started really seeing some money: the streets.

TRANSITIONS

I first became aware of what drugs were around the time I was seven or eight years old. In normal everyday society, drug use is hidden. For one thing, it's illegal. There are consequences that come with using drugs, not to mention a sense of shame amongst your family and friends. You're urged to go to rehab, sometimes forced. They stage interventions, confronting you about how your drug use is affecting them. It's possible to be ostracized, disowned and even disinherited for giving in to the dangerous, evil and costly habit of using narcotics. But things are different in the hood.

Drugs are very much a part of the culture in the hood. That's not to say that they're okay; they're not. But drugs are a substantial revenue stream in many impoverished urban areas in this country. They keep hundreds of thousands of young boys and girls seduced by the lure of fast money. These are kids who already feel disenfranchised by society. I should know - I was one of them. And since drug sales are a vital source of income in the hood, drug use is more acceptable. If Mc-

Donald's was the only restaurant in your neighborhood, you wouldn't necessarily be surprised by a rise in obesity. Drug use becomes so commonplace that it's easy to become desensitized. That is, until it's the person closest to you.

By 1985, I was a father and a successful hustler. I had enough work on the streets that my little girl Ashley was well taken care of, and I was becoming my mother's main source of income. I was also growing closer to my biological father Ernest Prince and his other children, my sister Ronda and my brother Thelton. At times Ernest's heroin addiction was manageable; other times it was overwhelming. But he'd been using since around the time I was born, so I'd never known who he was without it. My mother was different.

My sister's death and the stillborn baby were two of the things my mother never quite got over. I recently took a trip back to my childhood apartment – my first time since Zenia's accident – and I was overwhelmed by the emotions of simply returning to my bedroom on Coke Street. So I can't begin to imagine what it has been like for my mother all these years. The man I am now can understand all of the heartaches and trauma she endured in life, even while she was still a child herself. But the young man I was back then - a hardened street boss, a new father and someone who worshipped my mother - could only comprehend one thing: money came up missing.

By 21, I'd already saved $100,000 in street money. I bought my mother a four-bedroom house sitting on an acre of land. And a vacuum cleaner, too. I'd fulfilled my lifelong dream that began with the conversation I had with Zenia the night before she died. But I was also beginning to understand exactly how much it really cost me. My spirit was black.

To survive in the streets you have to play a constant game of mental toughness. There are a million different things coming at you from every angle, each trying to kill you. So you have to live as a predator because you won't survive as prey. Especially if you have a little bit of money.

When you have money in the hood, everyone tests you. They're either asking for money or they're trying to take it. So I became a savage. Numb. I knew what I was doing was wrong, but I couldn't allow myself to think about it. I had a goal: to lift my mother out of the impoverished world she was born into. I wanted her to finally feel freedom, to have hope again. She lost her childhood to raising me, so I wanted to give her some of those years back. And I was willing to die for it. I distanced myself, only hanging around people who were as savage as I was. I'd stopped going to church because I knew that if I faced God, I couldn't continue. But I had to continue. For her.

My mother's new house became a place of refuge; I didn't want to live anywhere else. I'd left the apartments on Coke Street long behind because I felt it was necessary for my survival, but I never wanted to leave her. And now I was back. I had $100,000 to my name and here I was, happy to be moving back in with my mother. Sure, I had girlfriends, but as far as I was concerned, nothing would ever separate me from my mother again. I'd worked too hard and sacrificed too much of my spirit for this. And then my mother's boyfriend moved in.

Her boyfriend and I didn't really get along, but he stayed out of my way, and he seemed like he made her happy, so I let him stay. At the time I was making a lot of other business moves. I'd learned a lot during my short tenure at the bank. There was an entire world out there operating by different financial standards. I started looking into different investment opportunities, partnering up with people I knew from all walks of life to make sure I always had money coming in. If there's anything I learned from my many childhood hustles it was to always have more than one. If none of my chickens were laying eggs, at least I had lawns to mow. And if the winter came early and my lawnmowing business dried up, I could always get a dice game going.

Adulthood wasn't much different. Even though I hung around people who dealt drugs and people who smoked drugs all day, every day, using drugs had never appealed to me. I had made up my mind at a young age that I wanted to be in control of my mind at all times. I'd only tried marijuana once, in the fourth grade, when one of the older guys on the block asked me to light his joint. I puffed on it and blew it out. I really didn't know what the hell I was doing, and I didn't like the way it tasted. I didn't see the benefit of it, and most of all, I felt that it was wrong. The lure to me was always the money. Cold, hard cash. It's that simple.

I was so good at saving money that I was stingy, even when I needed something for myself. I can recall one night as a child, waiting for my grandmother to get home because I was hungry. My stomach was grumbling so loud she could hear it when she came home; she cooked my favorite dish, rice and beans. I cleaned every inch of the plate. When I was finished eating, I picked my teeth and then pulled out a wad of cash out of my pocket and started counting. I love counting money, always have. I loved the way it felt in my pocket. I'd counted out about $75 before my grandmother noticed. "Who's money is that?" she asked. I told her it was mine; I was proud of my bankroll. She whooped me. Then, she told me, "Don't you ever get so stingy that you'd rather sit here and starve instead of spending a little money to get yourself something to eat!" But that was how much money meant to me. It represented freedom. Control.

Money. *Ahhhh*, it felt good not being broke. And it set me apart, because the people I was hanging around were always broke. I was addicted to the feeling of freedom. I loved the fact that I was improving my financial state every day. I became the provider in my mother's house. I retired her. It was an honor for me to be able to provide for someone who had provided for me all of my life. I felt a sense of accomplishment to be able to take care of her financial needs.

We could've gone on like that for forever. And we did, for almost three years. My mother had two more children, another boy and girl, and they too were being taken care of. I was in the streets most of the time, so it didn't make much difference if there were babies in the house. We had plenty of room.

My sister Ronda and I grew closer during this time. We'd always been cool, from the day we found out about each other. We share the same seriousness, although she may be a little more no-nonsense than I am. And she's as smart as a whip. We could relate to one another. She was on track to graduate high school and head off to college. I'd met my brother Thelton while I was still in high school. He wasn't a street guy, but the temptation was becoming hard for him to resist, and that was the last thing I wanted him to get into. He was a year younger than I was, and the only thing that held his attention was rap. He went by the name "Sir Rap-A-Lot." He was so serious about it that he'd gone out to Oakland, California to pursue his career. That didn't work out, but I could tell it was important to him, so I made him an offer. I told him I would build a studio for him to record his raps. He'd have full use of this studio as much as he wanted, for as long as he wanted, as long as he stayed out of the streets. He took the deal, and we built a studio at my car lot on Shepherd Street. That was how Rap-A-Lot Records was formed, in the end of 1986.

I listened to music, mostly rap and R&B, like everyone else. But my mind wasn't on turning it into a business. I made the offer because I cared about my brother. I didn't want to see him end up a statistic like so many other young guys. Eventually other guys began to hang out in the studio, laying down their verses. I'd drop by on a regular basis to listen, but also to get reports on my brother. I came across a couple teenagers, Keith "Sire Jukebox" Rogers and Oscar "Raheem" Ceres, who were trying to rap. I convinced their parents to let them move in with my good friend NC Trahan, a guy I'd known practically all my life, by assuring them that the guys would finish school while making their music. Now my brother was a part of a group; it wasn't just Sir Rap-A-Lot. We called them the Ghetto Boys.

In the beginning, NC was much more attentive to the music than I was. I had just had my third child, James Jr., and was focused on my street hustle. I'd started to notice pieces of jewelry turning up missing. One night I went to my safe to count my money - something I still did from time to time – and discovered more than a few dollars missing. I asked my mother if she knew anything about it, and she said she didn't, so I let it go.

Soon, a whole rack of jewelry went missing, and I put my ear to the streets. I was blatantly getting robbed; I couldn't keep ignoring what was going on in front of my face. Word got back to me that my property was over in the projects. Someone over there had some of my missing stuff. I pulled up and out of respect, the guy told me he wasn't the one stealing from me. He'd bought my jewelry in exchange for some rocks.

"Rocks" are what we call crack cocaine, which is a combination of cocaine, baking soda and ammonia. When heated and then cooled, it forms a solid lump, which can be broken up into smaller pieces: "rocks." When I asked my mother about it, she denied everything. More items continued to come up missing. Finally, one night, I caught her and her boyfriend red-handed.

Everything I'd done was for my mother. I'd put in so much work on the streets, enough to build a fortune, so that I could move her out of the projects and into our home. And now she was addicted to the same type of drug, to the point that she'd even steal from the home I'd bought her. My heart broke. The irony haunted me. All of the emotions I'd worked to numb began coming to life, one evil and painful deed at a time. That was the beginning of the end of James Smith. I changed my name to James Prince. I left my mother's house, never to return. Something had irrevocably broken between us. I still honored my mother because she gave me life and had given her all to raise me. But that bond I'd felt, that closeness, that allure she held over me, was now gone. Crack cocaine had come between us, as it did millions of other families in every hood throughout the country.

Look, I'm an intelligent man. I know how successful I was on the streets and I know what the odds are. I've asked myself a million times if there was a chance that it was my work that strung her out. It's an ugly question to have to ask yourself. And I struggled with the answer. Years later, my mother would tell me that she'd begun using crack cocaine long before that night, before I bought the house. Long before I was in the streets. Her drug use began when I was a child. Looking back on those years, I think a part of me always knew, but never wanted to admit it to myself. But there's no victory in knowing that it wasn't you that strung your own mother out. That's like standing over a corpse, happy that it wasn't your bullet that ended the life of someone you love. Semantics. In the grand scheme of things, they're still dead.

In some ways, my mother and I weren't that different. Hustling is an addiction too. Whether you're selling or using, it's the same. When a user is out of product, he's tweaking, geeking, he would do just about anything to get that high. When a dealer is out, he has the same feeling, but from a different perspective. He'll put his life on the line just to re-up.

And death was closing in on me. In the months that followed, I was a madman. I started spending more and more time in the studio because I needed something else to focus on. My hardened soul was thawing and every part of me felt it was on fire. I knew I'd crossed too many lines. I had enemies in the streets, waiting to see weakness in me. I'd become one of those kids I preyed on in school. I felt myself being watched. I knew they were looking for my vulnerabilities. Many of my friends were dying, being hunted down in the streets like animals. I was sure my phone was tapped, which usually means the Feds are listening. If they're listening, a case is coming.

I couldn't hide even if I wanted to. Everyone knew me. Everyone knew my cars, knew my hangout spots. I couldn't sleep, no matter how tired I was. The moment I closed my eyes, all the things I tried to forget came back in my mind, like a movie I never wanted to see. I was trapped. The only place I could breathe was in the studio. The Ghetto Boys weren't bad. I liked the feeling I had watching them work. It felt like something special. It felt like – with a lot of work – they could really be something. But in 1987, street dudes thought rappers were squares. We were making more money in the streets in one day than most rappers would see in a lifetime. And we owned ourselves. There was no label controlling us, no one standing between us and our money. The idea of going into rap full-time was a downgrade; a pay cut. It'd be a step down from being *the man*, but being *the man* came with a heavy price.

THE BIGGEST DEAL I EVER MADE

THE ART & SCIENCE OF **respect**

Before I went into the streets, I'd asked God for one thing: *before You take my life or take my freedom, give me a sign.* I felt like I was losing my mind, but I knew without question that the path I was on was leading to jail or the grave. God had given me the sign I'd asked for.

I had to make a choice. I could keep living with a short-term mentality, and if I was lucky, I could ball out for two or three or four more years, making more money than most people will ever see in their lifetime. But I knew if I chose to stick with the streets, I'd only have a few more years left.

If I gave up the streets, I'd have to walk away from all of those potential profits, not to mention the luxuries I already had. But maybe I had a chance to go legit. Rap was lame, but it was legal. And maybe if I could figure out how to do it my way, and create my own lane, it would be alright.

And that's how I ended up sitting on the floor of that closet, with my infant son in my lap, covered in my own sweat, and I talked to Him. "I hear you, God."

Everything would have to go. The money. The cars. The house that I'd bought myself after leaving my mother's. The circle of guys I was hustling with. Under the agreement I made with God, I chose to walk away and not return to certain aspects of the streets. That was my oath: that I could never contribute my time or my money to those facets of the streets again. I would walk away from absolutely everything. And if I did, He would bless me beyond my wildest expectations. I know it seems crazy to read. It feels a little crazy every time I say it. But consider this: look at where I am now.

I made my choice, opened that closet door and walked out ready to build my empire.

As far as I know, this is the
only picture that exists of
me as a baby.

I wanted to drop out of high school in the ninth grade, but I'd given my mother my word that I would stick with it and graduate for her. Here's proof that I kept my word.

Me and my brother Thelton, a.k.a. "Sir Rap-A-Lot." I got into the music business to keep him off the streets. This photo was taken at my Uncle Don's house in California. I'm holding Uncle Don's champion game rooster.

A red Mercedes-Benz 500 SEC was my second drop-top convertible. I bought it from Terry Carter in the late 1980s. Suge Knight is on trial now accused of running Terry over and killing him on the set of the movie *Straight Outta Compton* in 2015.

My first Rolls Royce, with the matching FILA warm-ups. Stuntin' on them fools in 1986.

My first Mercedes-Benz, in 1985.

Years later, in an interview, Master P talked about how seeing me in this full-length mink coat inspired him.

Me and my parents, Ernest Prince and Sharon Smith, in the early 2000s.

Big Chief, Dewey,
Ernest Prince, Harr
Blodget at the Ja
convention in A

Visiting my parents 1988, exercising my entrepreneurship.

Kickin' it with my firstborn, Ashley.

Three the hard way: NC Trahan, me, and Anthony Price in the 1980s.

Celebrating NC's birthday in the mid-80s with the homies. As you can see, all of us were having money. RIP to NC, Kenneth Parks, and Vincent Jones.

With my Little League teammates *(l-r)* Dewey Forker, Mel Johnson, the shortest one is me, James Johnson at the time, Tommy Jones, Victor Melbert, and the twins Robby and Bobby Benjamin. These guys, along with my coach, Mr. Hall *(pictured with us in the newspaper article below)*, taught me the importance of winning at just nine years old.

Profile of A Champ
The Tuffly Park Colts

By Ted Fuller

The Tuffly Park Colts finally st a game-as a matter of fact ey lost their only two games in e state playoff in Kermit, exas, where they played 7 mes for the state championship.

At the end of their season in e Key Athelete League the lts won their division with a 0 record. They beat Angleton d LaMarque to clinch the vision crown. After beating 5 t of their 7 games in the state ayoff they came in second ace in the state.

The Colts team is made up of boys ranging in ages 9-12. This the first time they have mpeted in open-base comtition which is opposed to the gular league play of tight-se.

On Monday evening six members of the Colts stopped by odel Cities Director Palmer wser, Jr.'s office to show m their appreciation for elping the team get to make the ip to Kermit, Texas in far west exas.

According to James Hall,

coach of the Colts the team was prepared to leave for the state championship and all the coaches and parents were trying to round up cars to take the boys when they found out they were short of transportation and also money they were finally referred to Mr. Bowser.

Palmer Bowser, Jr. got in contact with John White of PULL who consented to allow the team to use the organization's bus and Palmer made arrangements for the teams financial assistance because as he says, "I could understand how these boys felt. I have been in the same situation as a kid myself back in Louisiana where we had won a championship and couldn't make it to the playoffs because we didn't have any transportation. So when they called me and told me about these boys stranded out there in the park, I relived all those memories and had to help them."

After showing Palmer Bowser, Jr. their trophy and telling him about how they won their division and how they came

in second in the state the six boys then left the talking to their coach, James Hall.

While James Hall was talking the boys seemingly had forgotten what they had come to this big office on the 19th floor on One Allen Center for. They were OOhing and AAhing about the scenery from the big floor to ceiling glass windows of the office and each one of them had to sit in Palmer's executive chair for size.

While the bo we wandering around e offi amazed at the scene y and e equipment James and Palmer were still talking about League and especially about the Colts. James Hall explained that the Colts were made up of bo s from Fifth ard d Kr mere arde Most them from around e area f Libe Road.

Thi week e Co ll play n the Hester House but they say it wi on for f "We are alr am

My sister Zenia, RIP.
Love you!

Me and the homie NC talking
race-car business in 1988.

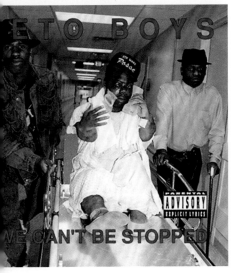

The Geto Boys' breakthrough album,
We Can't Be Stopped.

Dewey, Ray, me, and NC
partying in Dallas.

Lookin' straight into the camera with my mind on the money. 1987.

My first time meeting and interacting with Muhammad Ali. He was a scholar and a gentleman.

Kickin' it with my friends Salt-N-Pepa in the 1980s, before I made it in the music industry.

Both of these men above played a key role in my spiritual growth. On the left is Pastor C.L. Jackson and on the right is Pastor Ralph West. This event was the groundbreaking event for the Prince Complex Center, my boxing gym. Pictured below is the dedication ceremony for The James Andre Prince Chapel at The Church Without Walls.

Me and Big Chief visiting Larry Hoover in
prison in the mid-90s. As you can see, he
was dressed sharper than both of us.

Me and Don King kickin' game.

(Below) Boxers Roy Jones Jr., Ken Norton, and Buddy McGirt, track star Carl Lewis, Harold Dutton Jr., Gene Kilroy, my father Ernest Prince, and pastors Ralph Douglas West, C.L. Jackson, and Paul Jones were among those who came out to help me cut the ribbon at the Prince Complex groundbreaking ceremony.

At the top is my visitation with Diego Corrales in prison, and below is the meeting I arranged at my ranch with Mike Tyson and Roy Jones Jr. We met there to discuss a heavyweight fight between the two of them.

In California with Dr. Dre.

Me and Benzino and Dave Mays of *The Source* Magazine.

In the studio with Master P & Scarface.

In the studio with Cash Money's Birdman, Lil Wayne, & Juvenile.

A night out in Houston with Suge Knight after we struck a deal to release Tupac and Scarface's greatest hits. Unfortunately, Death Row's bankruptcy prevented the project from being released.

Puffy stopped by my ranch to visit me and my pet lion.

Eating good in Las Vegas with Chris Gotti, Kenneth "Supreme" McGriff, and Irv Gotti.

(Above) With Staye Down at Scarface's album release party in Houston.
(Below) At the 2004 Source Awards with Dave Mays, Benzino, Minister Farrakhan, Russell Simmons, & Suge Knight. *(Photo: Johnny Nunez/Getty Images)*

(Above) In Houston with Mama Wes, Lil Wayne, Bun B, Chamillionaire, & Z-Ro. *(Photo: Julia Beverly)*

(Below) Straight from the penitentiary to the Bentley dealership to get Pimp right. *(Photo: Omar Wilson)*

PART TWO:

WHO I BECAME

SEVEN YEARS

THE ART & SCIENCE OF respect

My goal was to have the type of lifestyle where I controlled my own time. I've never been someone who likes to get up early in the morning. When I was a kid, I hated getting up early to go to school. I'd observe all the different animals while I was walking to school – the dogs, the birds in the tree chirping – and they all had this peace about them. I wanted to be able to lay around and just relax like them. They were free. I didn't want to be under anyone else's control, and I wanted to be rich.

Even today, I don't wake up at any certain time. I wake up when all the sleep is out of my head. But I am very disciplined in other ways. For example, I only eat a meal once a day. I like having that structure and self-control to not just eat every time food is placed in front of me. I've read some Muslim literature which talks about how people a long time ago didn't abuse food like they do now, and they lived a lot longer and were a lot healthier. But, when I eat, I go in. I'm not a vegan or anything. I don't eat a lot of beef or pork, but I do eat beef and pork sometimes. I snack on fruit and nuts throughout my day.

I was able to accomplish my dream by creating a lifestyle that is complimentary to my work, and vice versa. No two days are the same. I'm mobile, my work is mobile. I travel the country several times a week. I wake up when I please and move around on my own time. I'm in love with serenity. Serenity is one of my favorite friends. I love peace. I don't like confusion. Anything that's opposite of serenity, I try to stay free from it. And I am a wealthy man. I also know that I am able to live this way because of the sacrifices and prayers that were made for me.

There is no such thing as an overnight success. A get-rich-quick scheme always ends with a negative outcome. I should know; I gave it all up. Remember?

After I'd made my decision, I downgraded from a five-bedroom house to a one-bedroom apartment in a matter of months. I unloaded my Mercedes-Benz and the rest of my luxury cars and became the proud owner of one Astro van. If it could be considered a luxury, I let it go. Instead I focused on one goal: Rap-A-Lot Records.

I started out with the first installment of the Ghetto Boys, which included Jukebox, Raheem, and my brother Thelton, who was Sir Rap-A-Lot at the time, but later changed his name to K9. My buddy NC helped me keep everything in line, while other guys like Richard Shaw, a three-foot-tall dwarf I met in a club, started hanging around, looking for ways to contribute and be down with the cause. We didn't have much of a structure yet but God had given me a sign that if I stayed the course, Rap-A-Lot Records would be a success. So I was willing to do whatever it took to get my label off the ground.

"Car Freak" was the Ghetto Boys' first single, a song about a girl who cared more about a guy's car than the guy who owned the car. I worked the nightclubs, getting the DJs to spin the record. It was bass-heavy and fell right in line with the songs they were already playing. It wasn't a breakout hit, but it set two important things in motion. For one, Raheem had enough charisma to go solo. A&M Records was interested in him, and this led to Rap-A-Lot Records' first nationwide distribution deal. The deal itself was worth $160,000, which I put right back into the label to pay for overhead, promotion, pressing up records and studio time. The other thing "Car Freak" did was attract a DJ out of Trenton, New Jersey who'd just moved to Houston and was looking for a place to make some music.

DJ Ready Red came to my car lot with my friend NC. I liked Red's DJ skills, and he saw my vision and really believed Rap-A-Lot was going to be a movement. We moved him into the room above the car lot, where he set up his Technics 1200 turntables and Roland 909 drum machine and went to work as the Ghetto Boys' official producer and DJ.

Having an in-house producer made all the difference. Red worked in that room day and night, making beats, coming up with song concepts and defining our sound. The artists, on the other hand, weren't working out as well. In the early days, the Ghetto Boys had a revolving door. Everybody wants to be a star, but nobody wants to work like a star. For every one year an artist is on top, you better believe there's been at least three years where they were struggling, trying to make ends meet while pushing toward their dreams. Not everyone is built to survive the struggle, no matter how talented they are. The hardest part is staying focused even when everything else around you is in chaos. As the leader of the movement, I had to constantly remind myself of that.

My days had become the same. I'd wake up around 11 AM, pray, go round up the guys and bring them to the studio, take whatever meetings we'd set up until nightfall, head out to the clubs looking for talent while trying to get the DJs to spin my records, then head back to the studio until daybreak, listening to the material they'd recorded that night. I'd fall asleep in bed around 6 AM, exhausted, but my mind still racing. It was a grueling grind, six days a week. I'd only take a break on Sundays to pick up my children, pile them in the van, and take them to church. Even though I was struggling, I was back in God's good graces, and church was a welcome refuge from the studio and all the pressures of running the label. Heavy is the head that wears the crown. God knew exactly what I was going through.

There were hard choices to make. My brother Thelton wanted to be a star, but he didn't want the countless hours of work it took to get there. By the time "Car Freak" was getting a little buzz, Thelton was already missing recording sessions, rehearsals, and meetings. If it was boring but important, he missed it. He'd gotten into drugs and was letting it distract him. I had to make a decision, so I dropped Thelton from the label. For years to come, my decision would remain a sore spot. After all, he was the reason I started the label in the first place. I've been asked several times over the years, "How do you do that to your own brother?" But that's also a question for Thelton. No one owes you anything, so if you find someone willing to take a chance on you, it's on you to deliver. It's a lot harder to find someone willing to take a *second* chance on you.

My family wasn't happy about Thelton getting dropped from the label, but they didn't know what to make of Rap-A-Lot in the first place. For a poor family from Texas in the 1980s, the world of entertainment was completely foreign. They didn't know anyone in the rap business; that world only existed on television and on the radio. It certainly didn't exist in Fifth Ward. As far as they were concerned, I was wasting my time.

I'd walked away from the streets, and it was tough trying to turn a profit at a car lot. I was barely making enough to keep the lights on. Some of my family members told me to "be normal": go out and find a job like everybody else. But I'm anything but normal. And thank God He gave me enough sense not to try to pretend like I was.

My entire life, I'd been known as the guy who had money. I'd always kept a bankroll, even as a small child. But 1988 was the first time I was broke. I was living in debt. The label was costing more money than it was earning. Even the bare necessities, like paying utility bills on time, were starting to feel like luxuries. People who knew me were puzzled. I'd disconnected myself from a lot of my street homies to become more focused. I didn't tell many people about my breakthrough in the closet. To the outside world, I'd simply chosen to go from being hood rich to dead broke.

It was around this time, six months or a year into my Rap-A-Lot days, when I ran into a buddy of mine from my street days. My pockets were empty, and he knew it. He gave me his number and told me if I ever needed anything, I could call him. In other words, he had a line on some money. Some real money. I carried that piece of paper with me for a few days. I knew if I made that one phone call, within a week I'd have enough money to pay for everything Rap-A-Lot needed. I could pay all the bills and move into a better place. I knew I'd be taking a step in the wrong direction. That piece of paper started to feel like lead, weighing my pockets down, distracting me from the promise I'd made to God and the work I had before me. By the fourth day, I'd had enough. I stopped at a red light, tore up his phone number, and tossed the pieces of paper out of my window. Eventually, I knew I'd give in to temptation and call him, so I had to distance myself and focus on my purpose.

Right away I saw the value in having as much studio time as possible. The more time the guys spent making music, the better they became. Red was able to make beats in our makeshift studio, but we needed to record at a place with proper equipment. And studio time cost money. A lot of money.

One day I was sitting in my car lot when a truck rolled up, stacked high with furniture and suitcases. Out climbs this blond-haired, blue-eyed white guy looking for me. At first, I thought he was the Feds, but he wasn't. His name was Cliff Blodget, and he was an engineer from Seattle. He'd come to Houston on a mission. He heard there was a brand new music scene, so he packed up all of his worldly possessions and drove down to get in on the ground floor. Someone pointed him in my direction.

We set Cliff's equipment up in the same room as Red, and by the end of the day we had our own studio. Red called a buddy of his in

Trenton, Prince Johnny C, who came down to try out for the Ghetto Boys. Their first album, *Making Trouble*, didn't make the most noise but it showed growth and consistency, which is important when you're building a fanbase. As long as you're putting out product on a regular basis, showing improvement each time, your fanbase will grow. Most importantly, it was enough to get Houston included in the rap conversation. Before that album, nobody was talking about the South. That release gave my city hope that more was on the way.

Cliff became my partner in Rap-A-Lot and added the business structure that we needed to match my hustling mentality. He held down the studio, which allowed me the freedom to get out there on the road and make sure our music was getting in the right hands. Before the internet, there wasn't the option to email or download a file. In those days, if you wanted someone to have your music, you had to give him or her a cassette tape or wax. Or if you wanted DJs to play it, you had to meet them face to face. The entire thing took a lot of time, energy, and resources, and we were figuring out most of it as we went along.

Cliff and I had different visions for the growth of the company. He was concerned with making art. I wanted art that made money. I'm not a musician. I'm not a writer. I'm not an artist. I'm an entrepreneur. My masterpiece is my bank account.

One night at a nightclub, I was approached by a tall, skinny white boy with blond hair. He looked goofy. But then he got up to dance. I'd never seen a white boy with those kind of moves, and I was intrigued. At the end of the night he came back to my studio with me and played some of his music, and there was one song in particular that stood out. I can't remember if it included the sample yet, but I'll never forget that hook: *Ice, ice, baby. Vanilla Ice, ice, baby.* I told Cliff that night, "Sign him."

Robert Van Winkle, "Vanilla Ice," was an aspiring rapper out of Dallas, and for a week or two in 1989, he camped out at my studio working on music. This wasn't unusual. There were dozens of rappers who hung around the studio, who were either already signed to Rap-A-Lot or hoping to get signed. At the time, I wasn't as focused as I should've been. I relied on Cliff to run the company's day-to-day operations. I was in the studio at night with the artists until 6 or 7 AM every morning. Everyone showed up to the studio because of me. I was the producer because I brought everyone together to make music. They came, stayed, and worked because of my presence, and I knew that.

There's a feeling you get when you hear a hit for the first time. It changes your emotions in one of two ways - it makes you think or makes you want to dance. When the radio station played "Ice Ice Baby" back to back, I was smiling from ear to ear. I raced to the nearest phone to call Cliff. We did it! I knew Vanilla Ice was going to be a monster, and he belonged to Rap-A-Lot.

...But Cliff had never signed him. He didn't think Vanilla Ice was worth the trouble. Rob and his manager Tommy Quon had done a deal with Ichiban instead. We'd lost out, big time.

Although I can blame Cliff, I can't blame Cliff. I wasn't on top of my business like I should've been. I wanted Vanilla Ice signed and should've followed up, checked in on the project, made sure it was headed in the right direction. Even if Cliff had signed him like I asked, who knows if the song would've still found that bassline from Queen's "Under Pressure"? It might not have even been a hit. In any case, Vanilla Ice briefly shook up the world, and "Ice Ice Baby" went multi-platinum both here and abroad.

Cliff did have some ideas on gaining commercial success. In 1989 we signed two acts, Royal Flush and Def IV. Cliff and Red both were excited about both acts, which they hoped would appeal to the mainstream. For one, they weren't gangster rappers. There was nothing hardcore about their music. And second, none of them were from the South. Def IV's members were from Brooklyn and Chicago, and Royal Flush hailed from New York.

Cliff had one more idea. He wanted to move Rap-A-Lot to New York. We set up shop in a two-story house in Huntington, New Jersey, which felt like a foreign land. To me, it didn't feel like Rap-A-Lot, but Cliff, Red, and the artists insisted that this was what we needed. New York was the center of the music business, and certainly the mecca for rap music at that time. They thought by tapping into those resources, we'd find commercial success.

We didn't find anything. We got lost. But one good thing did come out of our time in New York: I reconnected with Lyor Cohen, a young music manager from Rush Management and Def Jam Records. He talked fast, with a deep, Israeli accent. Lyor Cohen knew how to command a room without making anyone feel less important. I liked him. I'd met him a few years prior at a Run-DMC concert and we stayed in touch. And now that I was in New York, I wanted to spend as much time with him as possible. Me and Lyor was cool, and he picked up the phone whenever I called. I spent as much time as possible in the Def Jam office, soaking up the atmosphere, observing the different departments. I hung around so much that eventually they started showing me the checks. I'll never forget looking at the check for an LL Cool J project for $200,000 and thinking to myself, *Wow, they're getting money like this?*

The time I was able to spend in the Def Jam offices nearly made up for the time we'd gotten off track by moving to New York. That connection with Lyor was a blessing. He answered all my questions and gave me some great advice. Watching everyone in the Def Jam office filled me with inspiration. They had their own swagger and they were at home in their own world. And here we were – a bunch of country guys from Houston – trying to fit in. I'd never been a follower, and I wasn't about to start now. Cliff and Red thought I was crazy when I decided to move back to Houston. My artists thought I was sabotaging their career, but I had to follow my gut. Rap-A-Lot was supposed to be about Houston. We couldn't be about Houston from New York. I told everyone to pack up, and we bounced.

As soon as we got back home to Houston, I called a meeting and told everyone point blank, "This is my last piece of money. I see what you're trying to do, but I done tried this your way. And now we're going to do this my way." I started writing. I'd sit in the studio with them all night long, writing out ideas and using actual lines from my life. I told the guys their job was to make it rhyme for me. I talked about where I was coming from and what I was going through. I wanted the public to relate to the Ghetto Boys because I was one of them, and I knew there were lots of other people out there like me. Rap-A-Lot was a hardcore rap label, representing the Houston sound. Moving forward, I expected everyone to go in the direction I wanted us to go.

Prince Johnny C and Jukebox both had problems with the new hardcore direction, which they thought was too deep. So I cut everyone from the Ghetto Boys except DJ Ready Red and Little Billy, who was now going by "Bushwick Bill." I was in the barbershop getting a haircut when my barber Harvey said there was a kid I should meet. Willie Dennis was a quiet but serious guy. He was young, no more than 23 years old, and built more like a boxer than a rapper. But he could rhyme.

A few weeks later I was leaving a club one night and passed a few guys in the parking lot who were listening to a young kid rap. The boy was nice, and I just walked up on him and asked him his name. He went by the name DJ Akshen, and I asked him right there if he wanted to roll with Rap-A-Lot. But he was signed to Shortstop Records, which was owned by an artist named Lil Troy (who would have a hit of his own ten years later with "Wanna Be A Baller"). DJ Akshen was real loyal to his crew. I offered to take him and his producer, Bido, to breakfast so we could talk. We sat in Denny's until the sun came up. I saw a lot of myself in Akshen. He told me he was tired of hustling, and felt like he was risking his life every time he tried to make a dollar. I understood him, and I also understood the dilemma he was in as an artist. Akshen was signed to Lil Troy's label for a single deal. I knew Troy; he used to work as a valet and park my cars when I came to the club. So I told DJ Akshen to let Troy work the single they'd recorded together and let me record his album, and I went to go talk to Lil Troy myself to make sure there were no hard feelings.

I went to meet with Lil Troy by myself. He had more than a handful of his homies there, one of whom was cutting hair. I sat down and got myself a cut, and while I was in the chair, I explained my plan for DJ Akshen. "He's a talented young brother, and I can do way more for him than you can at this point," I said. I told him I wanted Akshen to honor his single deal with Troy – I even offered to help them promote the song – and then Akshen would come record his album and the Ghetto Boys album with Rap-A-Lot. I explained to Troy that I'd come there to ask his blessing to move forward with his artist. Troy looked me in my eye and gave his consent.

Later that night, DJ Akshen and his producer came running to my office. They told me that Troy was threatening their lives and had put them out of the place they were staying. I knew right then the type of man I was dealing with. I told DJ Akshen that he was with me now, and I was with him, and from this day forward I would fight his battles. And if he had any more trouble with Lil Troy or anyone else, they'd have trouble with me.

I had heard the 12" single DJ Akshen was planning to work. It was good, but Cliff and Red put their own touches on it and gave it a more Rap-A-Lot sound. The last thing was his name. We were a hardcore rap label. This kid was good, and I knew he was the voice and the lyrical force we needed. I thought his name should match his deep, throaty voice and his dark content. His single was called "Scarface," so it was only right that he take the same name.

That's how Willie D, Scarface, and Bushwick Bill ended up in the studio with DJ Ready Red, working on what would become *Grip It! On That Other Level.* The music was hard. The lyrics was dark, borderline scary. But I knew we had something. The album debuted at #166 on the Billboard 200 chart and #19 on the Top R&B/Hip Hop Chart. It had taken several years, but we finally had our first taste of success. But as we continued to push the record, I realized that we had a problem. The radio stations in Houston were monopolized by the East Coast DJs.

For a long time, East Coast DJs had a stronghold on our clubs and radio stations. They only played East Coast music. They criticized our Southern accents, they criticized our sound, and they were blatantly working against our movement. Although I was impressed by their unity, I realized I had to do something about it.

First, I asked them nicely to play our records. I'd give them a courtesy call and ask them to get behind the Houston movement and give the artists a chance to be heard. If the public didn't like the artists' music, I would have accepted that, but they weren't even giving us a chance.

Asking nicely wasn't getting us anywhere, so ultimately, we had to demand our respect. And when you demand respect, it's not always pretty. To make a long story short, a lot of the East Coast DJs decided to move out of Houston because they were no longer wanted here.

I heard a story about a program director on the southwest side of Houston who was controlling the airwaves at the time. Some of the public had to make themselves known to him. Rap-A-Lot had so much love in the streets that these guys actually put an ass-whupping on this program director to let him know that they wanted to hear Rap-A-Lot.

Radio is not as pretty as it sounds. Radio stations are a playing field where gangstas play, and they do a lot of things that you all may be unaware of. So don't feel sorry for them, and don't hold back. Push your music by any means necessary. It has to be done strategically, but the point is, we had to fight. I fought for Houston music to be heard, and we eventually won the war. We blazed a trail. It didn't happen by itself.

Sometimes when I observe what's going on in Houston today, I'm disappointed to see things returning to the old way, not allowing the youth to be heard. Whether you're in Houston or anywhere else in the world, you have to come together and create a movement. Fight for your records to be heard. You deserve that chance. Your family deserves to eat too, but you have to fight for it. It's not going to just fall into your lap.

Ultimately, it would take seven years of developing Rap-A-Lot for me to get back where I'd been financially on the night of my breakthrough. I sacrificed a lot during those seven years. Those were some of the hardest years of my life, but they were also some of the most important. My belief system and my faith got me through. Anyone who's ever set out to do something great will tell you that the road is paved with potholes of self-doubt, plenty of detours, and numerous roadblocks. Even when everyone doubted me or told me I was doing the wrong thing, I listened to my inner voice. My spirit told me I would make it through and succeed. But the path to success is never easy.

After we kicked in the doors for Houston with the Ghetto Boys, I let my other artists run through the doors and eat with us. Over the years, our roster would grow to include Ganksta N-I-P, The Terrorists, the Odd Squad and Devin the Dude, Blac Monks, DMG, A G 2 A Key, OG Style, Choice, the Ghetto Twinz, Big Mike, Yukmouth, 3-2, the 5th Ward Boyz, Z-Ro, Pimp C and Bun B, Facemob, 5th Ward Juvenilez, Trae and Assholes by Nature, CJ Mac, Papa LQ, Dirty, Do or Die, Hi-C, Hussein Fatal and the Outlawz, Juvenile and UTP, Menace Clan, Almighty RSO, Partners in Crime, Seagram Miller, Snypaz, Too Much Trouble, 2 Low, and many others.

So the Ghetto Boys' breakthrough *Grip It! On That Other Level* was just the beginning. It brought us nationwide attention and helped Rap-A-Lot grow, but that attention also put us on the radar of a lot of people who wanted to shut us up.

GHETTO TO GETO

THE ART & SCIENCE OF
respect

The new Ghetto Boys lineup was a blend of interesting characters with colorful personalities who had already been through a lot in their lives. Willie D was born in the Fifth Ward to alcoholic parents. He often talked about the abuse he suffered at the hands of his mother and how that affected him as a child. Scarface had dealt with depression as a child; he'd tried to commit suicide, and often joked about making another attempt. Bushwick Bill was a Jamaican dwarf with a drug and alcohol problem. What did America expect them to talk about in their records? *Grip It! On That Other Level* was certified gold, but it still hadn't reached the mainstream masses.

Rick Rubin, the pioneer behind Def Jam Records, had literally started a record label in his dorm room at NYU. Rick and I were similar because he was always into doing things his own way. He wanted to stay on the cutting edge, no matter the cost.

In 1988, when his Def Jam business partner Russell Simmons refused to back the heavy metal band Slayer, Rick took the rights to Slayer and departed to start his own label. Rick's Def American Recordings was based in Los Angeles, and they'd secured a distribution deal with Geffen Records. Their roster included heavy metal acts Slayer, Danzig, The Four Horsemen, and the comedian Andrew Dice Clay.

Rick reached out to me and set up a meeting to talk about signing the Ghetto Boys, and he was very convincing in person. This was a man who had literally helped create the rap music business, so I knew he knew what he was talking about. But what attracted me most to Rick wasn't his Def Jam history, or his Def American present. It was the Geffen machine.

Rappers like Schooly D out of Philadelphia and Ice-T and N.W.A on the West Coast were selling out shows, but their hardcore lyrics were also upsetting conservatives, ministers, and even black comedians like Bill Cosby. Many people felt that the hardcore rap was glorifying violence, reinforcing harmful stereotypes, causing misogyny and racism, and having a bad influence on children. But we were just talking about the things we knew. It's interesting when your reality offends someone else's idea of what your reality *should* be.

Meanwhile, back in Houston, the guys weren't getting along. Scarface, Willie D, and Bushwick were always very different people with very different personalities. I put them in the group because of their individual talents, not because of a synergy between them. There was a lot of tension between them, and it seemed like every other day we were breaking up a fight. But somehow, it only made the music better. We were finally making some money, and they were starting to see their efforts pay off.

Rick Rubin knew we had something special, and he wanted to be a part of it. We agreed to sign a deal where the Ghetto Boys would be signed to Def American through Rap-A-Lot. Rick Rubin was now back in the rap business, and Rap-A-Lot now had access to the Geffen Records machine. We all got to work immediately. The plan was to repackage *Grip It! On That Other Level* as a self-titled major label debut, along with two new songs. Rick was anti-establishment, and he liked the fact that we didn't hold back lyrically. He wanted to add to our movement. The first thing we did was change the spelling of the group's name from Ghetto to Geto. "Ghetto" was in the dictionary, so it wasn't our word. It belonged to the establishment. "Geto" belonged to us.

The momentum was building as we approached the October 1990 release date. We'd shot the album cover, which featured each member in a mugshot. Then, less than two months away from the release, I got a call from Rick. Geffen was pulling out of the deal. They refused to distribute the album, describing it as "violent and dangerous." This was exactly the kind of politics Rick hated. He was against censorship as much as I was against anyone telling me what I could and couldn't do with my own music. But Geffen was firm. They were fine with distributing satanic metal bands like Slayer, but considered *us* too offensive. So Rick took his record label and all of his artists, including the Geto Boys, over to Geffen's parent company, Warner Bros.

It was Rick Rubin's idea to add this warning label to the front of every CD: "Def American Recordings is opposed to censorship. Our manufacturer and distributor, however, do not condone or endorse the content of this recording, which they find violent, sexist, racist, and indecent." The Geto Boys went gold. The controversy was the greatest free promotion we could've ever gotten.

Over the years, I've listened to many people criticize rap music without ever discussing ways to improve the environment which birthed us. I've learned that America is okay with us living in these conditions, as long as the rest of them don't have to hear about it. I wasn't going to apologize for where I'm from and I wasn't going to hide it. Right or wrong, this is how we grew up, on the margins of society.

In the midst of all the controversy, Rick Rubin went to David Geffen and asked to be released from his distribution deal. Rick had every right to do what was best for his own company. And David Geffen, respecting Rick as a businessman, released Def American Recordings from their deal. To Rick, it was a matter of principle. To me, it was a matter of money. I'd signed the Geto Boys to Def American because I wanted to be closer to the Geffen Records marketing machine; I'd admired they way they did business and wanted a piece of that success. But I didn't come to Rick to end up somewhere else. So I asked to be released.

It was hard getting Rick on the phone after that conversation. He went radio silent on me for a couple months. Finally, I had to have some associates of mine get next to him and put a phone to his ear. David Geffen respected Rick Rubin enough as a businessman to allow him to go where he felt was best for his company, and I felt that Rick needed to show me that same respect. I believe in standing up for our rights to free speech and fair business. So Rap-A-Lot parted ways with Def

American after only one album.

When your home phone rings at 3 AM, it means something's wrong. I got a call telling me that there had been a confrontation, a gun went off, and Bushwick had been shot in his eye. I just knew he was dead. That's all I kept thinking. *He's got to be dead.* But he wasn't.

By the time the story hit the morning news, Bushwick had lost his eye, but everything else about him seemed pretty Bushwick Bill. The politicians had a field day with that one: "Here's another example of how the Geto Boys advocate senseless violence." We didn't advocate senseless violence.

Bushwick Bill had gotten drunk off of Everclear and done something really, really stupid, and he paid for it with his right eye. But we didn't shy away from it. We already knew what our haters would say, and we were about telling the truth, raw and uncut. We called a photographer, sent Willie D and Scarface home to get changed, and the next day we removed Bushwick's bandages and wheeled him into the hallway at the hospital for a photo shoot. It was our way of saying, "Yes, this really happened, America. Deal with it."

The picture became the cover of the Geto Boys' next album, *We Can't Be Stopped.* Propelled by the single "Mind Playing Tricks on Me," it was the first Rap-A-Lot album to go platinum. It was fitting for this to be the song that catapulted Rap-A-Lot into platinum territory, because it was the real-life story behind the song that set the movement into motion in the first place. The song was written by Scarface, and it was based on the days leading up to my breakthrough in the closet where I made a pact with God. With or without Geffen, Def American, or the agreement of any politician or activist, Rap-A-Lot Records was a bona fide movement. And just like the album title, there was no stopping us.

FROM REVELATION TO MANIFESTATION

I've always wanted a ranch, ever since I was a small child riding to the penitentiary to visit my uncle. We'd pass the lush, green land in my grandmother's car, and even as a little boy, I knew that only God could make something like that. I wanted my own piece of it. I became fixated on the idea of owning property. In my high school drafting class, I would always create big, elaborate houses, sitting on more land than the eye could see. The more I drew it, the realer it became.

By the time I was 23 years old, I was in the streets heavy and had saved enough money to buy myself a house sitting on 30 acres of land. It felt like my own piece of heaven. More importantly, I'd accomplished a longtime goal. The ranch allowed a respite from the rest of my life. It became my place of peace where I'd go think and spend time in solitude. I kept that ranch for a few years, but after a while I felt like I was outgrowing it. I was no longer in the streets, Rap-A-Lot was becoming profitable, and my life was changing. I was changing. I was grateful for those 30 acres, but I'd outgrown it. My spirit needed more land. I reached out to a realtor, and the hunt began.

For weeks, the realtor took me to ranch after ranch. I told her I didn't have a budget, I just wanted to find a plot of land that I loved. My instructions were simple: "Find me the nicest plot of land with 100 acres or more." For months we looked at properties, but everything she showed me was just okay. She took me to a 600-acre ranch about an hour outside of Houston, which was beautiful, but it didn't feel like *mine*. We were both getting frustrated with the process. Finally I told her, "Look, I'm looking for something that takes your breath away." I asked her to take me to the nicest property she could find.

Finally, we rode out to the Diamond-A Ranch, a thousand-acre property about 45 minutes outside of the city. I was speechless as I walked through the beautiful Spanish-style home, which sat on a lake full of bass, catfish, and turtles. For months, I'd been asking her to show me nothing but the best, but she had been taking me to mediocre properties. I asked her why. "I didn't think you wanted to spend this much money," she said.

Despite repeatedly telling her that I had an unlimited budget for the right property, my agent, a white woman, had sized me up and put a cap on my dreams even when I hadn't. We began negotiations with the owner of the property.

In the meantime, I'd been speaking with my pastor Ralph West about his plans to expand The Church Without Walls. Their plans were ambitious, and they would need help to pull it off. While waiting for the ranch sale to be approved, I found myself at a church meeting about the expansion. There were some very real concerns about a realistic construction timeline. Since their income depended on church members, there was concern about running out of money mid-construction. I didn't want to see the church risk bankruptcy. The amount they needed to complete the entire expansion - $1 million dollars - was the same amount I was preparing to pay as the down payment on my new ranch.

I looked around at the church, which had been so good to me over the years, and I thought about the irony of the situation. Without God's grace, I wouldn't have a million. I wouldn't even still be sitting here. "Let's build the entire thing," I told them. The church officials didn't really know me, so they didn't think I was serious until Pastor West spoke up and told them that I was a man of my word. A lot of people rejoiced, and others were in disbelief.

The church had a blueprint for Phase One and Phase Two of their construction plan. Phase One was for the adult sanctuary, and Phase Two was a second floor for children. The church only had enough money to begin Phase One. But God had other plans, and he moved me to complete Phase Two as well.

As I watched the church break grounds on the new facilities, there was no way I could regret my decision. It was a sacrifice, but I knew that I'd done the right thing. To my surprise, Pastor West honored me by naming the chapel outside of the sanctuary the James Andre Prince Chapel. I was grateful for the honor, and an elder in the church reminded me that I would need to be more conscious of my actions now that my name was on the church. This caused me to rethink some things moving forward.

Even though I had given away my intended down payment, I still kept the faith. I started regularly driving out to the Diamond-A Ranch just to ride by and look at the property. It was a peaceful ride; there was a sense of tranquility there that I really enjoyed. I got a sense of healing just by being out there on the three-mile stretch of the private road outside the perimeter. I'd take my family and friends there and tell them, "This is going to be ours." Seeing the property on a regular basis kept it fresh in my mind. It gave me a tangible goal to work towards.

Another thing that had a powerful effect on my life was the book *Think and Grow Rich*. It was given to me by a friend named Kim Harris, who was in law school at the time, and his simple gesture changed my life. It was written by Napoleon Hill during the Great Depression, but the principles of business are still applicable. To this day it remains one of the most successful books on personal growth and development. I read that book from cover to cover, and it helped bring structure to my life and my business. By reading other people's stories, I was able to identify with them. It helped me discover my gifts and taught me the importance of prioritizing my goals. It changed my way of thinking and inspired me to get organized. Rap-A-Lot was growing, but we were at a pivotal point. We could either keep growing to unprecedented levels, or it could all fall apart. I wanted to be revolutionary. When I finished reading that book I fell to my knees, asking God to give me clarity and a plan. One of the things Napoleon tells you to do in the book is to list out your goals. So I sat down with a notebook and then numbered my top ten goals. Most of the goals were ones I'd had in my head for many years, like becoming a millionaire outside of

Rap-A-Lot.

It's a blessing to have a lot of money, but as I'd learned from my numerous childhood hustles, you never have just one. I didn't want my wealth to be tied to Rap-A-Lot, so I needed to find other lucrative business ventures to add to my portfolio. Over the years I've tried many different things. I've had a number of successful ventures, such as Strapped, a condom company I created to promote sexual health in the urban community. I've also owned a limousine service for several years, which was a joint venture with my sister Ronda. Of course, as any entrepreneur will tell you, I've taken some substantial losses. I put a lot of money into a clothing line that never worked out for me. But with each venture, I learned a little bit more about how to do business - and how *not* to do business. But on that afternoon in 1993, I wrote down the list of my ten goals, and I knew that my spirit was in tune. I could envision myself accomplishing each one of these goals as I wrote them down.

Up until that point, I'd relied heavily on my partner Cliff Blodget to help navigate Rap-A-Lot from a homegrown independent company into the big leagues. Cliff had come along at just the right time. Not only was he the missing element of an engineer/producer with all the right recording equipment, but he provided a business structure at a time when we sorely needed it.

After reading *Think and Grow Rich* and analyzing our business structure, I realized where Rap-A-Lot was losing money. When I looked at our wins versus our losses, there was a clear pattern. It had taken a few years for us to achieve our first big radio record, and during that time, Cliff had done several business deals that weren't fruitful. It was becoming clear to me that when I followed someone else's decisions, we lost money, but when I followed my gut, we turned a profit. So I set up a meeting with Cliff.

I told Cliff that I wanted to take control of Rap-A-Lot's day-to-day administration. Cliff didn't think I was qualified or prepared to take on the role. I'd never kept regular office hours, but this felt like the right decision. He was even more upset when I told him that I was firing 90% of the staff, keeping only the essential positions. Now that I understood the value of having the right personnel, I didn't want to waste resources on staff we didn't need. Cliff told me I had no track record of running a company that size, and he was right. But he forgot one thing: I did have a track record of *building* a company that size.

The thing that upset Cliff the most was that I was making all of these radical and risky changes based on a prayer. He couldn't understand how I could value a word from God over facts right in front of my face. He left the meeting livid.

That's the hardest, and perhaps the most important, part of moving in faith. Your vision is your vision. All of my life I'd encountered people who weren't able to see my vision, and if I'd listened to them, I never would've been in a position to have this conversation with Cliff in the first place.

But I didn't need Cliff to understand my vision. I only needed to make sure he couldn't stop me. Since we couldn't come to an agreement, we only had two choices: we could dissolve the company, or I would have to buy him out. I'd come too far to quit now, so we struck a deal where Cliff received an undisclosed amount of money, and I walked away with my artists, my masters, and my name.

Plenty of my business associates told me I was making a mistake. They said I'd be bankrupt within six months. I didn't listen. I got rid of everyone except for four key people, and we went to work. I combined everything I'd learned from *Think and Grow Rich* with what I already knew from the streets. For the first time, I was in complete control of Rap-A-Lot, and it felt great. Within six months, we'd established the biggest profit margin in the history of Rap-A-Lot Records. And just one year later, I negotiated the most lucrative distribution deal in our history. Even Cliff would have to agree that I made the right decision.

Taking control of my company was a total leap of faith. I had done my homework, but the outcome – like any outcome – was yet to be determined. I had to rely on my faith and my work ethic. As I watched everyone file into The Church Without Walls for the dedication of the newly renovated facilities, I was proud of the decision I made. It was bigger than me. I put the needs of the people over the wants of my own, and I knew I'd done the right thing.

When Rap-A-Lot closed on the lucrative distribution deal, I sat down to look at my own personal stake. I no longer had a partner, which meant that I shouldered all of the risk but also pocketed all of the reward. So I called my realtor and made an even better offer on the Diamond-A Ranch. Today, it's known as the Prince Estates.

I was really attracted to the ranch from a business perspective because it pays for itself. It generates $200,000 every year from hay and black Angus cattle. So I was actually purchasing a ranch with a business attached. One of my biggest clients was the Houston racetrack. All of my life, I thought the only way to make money off grass was by selling weed – until I started selling hay. I think hay is a bigger business than the weed business. Producing the volume of hay we sell is a full-blown job, but there was already an existing infrastructure with a manager and employees when I bought the new ranch.

My faith had come full circle. With two of my goals checked off the list, now it was time to accomplish the eight others.

LARRY HOOVER

THE ART & SCIENCE OF respect

"You see, niggas in the street gotta get together all over the nation. We gotta get together in Chicago, we gotta get together in LA. We gotta get together in Houston. We gotta get together in New York. We gotta get together in Detroit. Niggas got to get together all over this nation. I'm talkin' bout not the regular people, I'm talkin' bout street niggas. I'm talkin' about niggas that call themselves gangstas. Real gangstas go to the polls. That's what's going to make the difference, too. That's that sleeping giant. That's that 40% apathetic vote within our black community. That's who we need to rise. That's who we need to awaken. They scared of me because I'm trying to wake that sleeping giant. See, these young brothas, they pay attention to what I say because I'm one of them. I understand where they been. I come from where they come from. I'm where they going to be if they don't watch what they do-ing." - *Larry Hoover (from the Geto Boys' 1996 album* Resurrection*)*

By 1993, we were spending more time on the road. Houston was showing love, but it was nowhere near what we were seeing in other cities, particularly in the Midwest. We were building our reputation as street guys, talking about things that real street guys go through. This hit home in places like Cleveland, Detroit, and Chicago, which is similar to Houston in some ways. The shine of the big city sometimes casts a big shadow over the hood. And just like Houston, Chi-Town had its own flavor, its own talk, and its own sound.

The streets of Chicago also had their own movement in the Gangster Disciples. I was invited to meet with one of the founders, the notorious Larry Hoover, who was serving a 200-year sentence at Dixon Correctional Center outside of Chicago. I'd never spoken with him before and didn't think he knew much about me, but I went, both out of curiosity and respect.

When you visit someone in a maximum-security jail, it's normal to sign in and be searched. But this time, when I visited Larry, a badge was clipped on me. I was told it was their new standard-issue visitor's badge.

I spent a little over an hour with Larry. He wore a Coogi sweater, slacks, and alligator shoes; he looked like someone lounging at home in his living room, not someone bound to spend the rest of their natural life behind bars. His body was locked up, but his mind remained free.

Throughout our conversation, I realized that this was a smart man who cared deeply about the streets and the people in them. I was surprised by how much he knew about me. We talked about my movement, and I explained that I wanted to use Rap-A-Lot to put the South on the map the same way the East Coast and the West Coast were on the map. I felt like we were being discriminated against; people looked down on our music and its "country" sound. I wanted the South to have our own voice and have the same respect as the East and the West.

Larry understood my desire to have a voice. Gangs are never made up of satisfied people. It doesn't matter if it's an Irish gang in the 19th century, a motorcycle gang in the 1970s, or a P Stone Ranger on the streets of Chicago in the 1990s - they all have one thing in common. They've gathered with other like-minded individuals because they wanted to be heard. There are many billion-dollar industries which started out as a criminal enterprise, and many of them were founded and controlled by gangs. Those gangs figured out how to offer a product which served the general public; an opportunity to go legit. We call it "going straight."

At the time I met with Larry, the DEA had already been investigating me for five years or more (we'll get to that story later). We talked about how it felt to have the government actively trying to destroy you. It was probably one of the most passionate topics we talked about during our visit. Larry knew all too well what I was going through and offered the best advice he could. "Just don't stop swinging at them," he told me. That's what I remember the most about that visit: a man sentenced to die in jail, telling me not to stop swinging.

A couple years later, the federal government brought more charges against Larry. They claimed he'd been running a "criminal enterprise" from behind bars. During his trial, it was revealed that the visitor's badge they clipped on me was actually a recording device. They'd been monitoring every one of his conversations in an effort to bring more charges against him. Larry was convicted again and sentenced to six life terms in federal prison, on top of the 200 years he was already serving. I guess they thought someone with such a strong voice was planning to live longer. I sincerely hope that someone with the right tools reads this and is able to correct this injustice. I call it an "injustice" because it was entrapment, and they had no legal standpoint to record our conversations. They violated our rights and invaded our privacy, and I hope that one day those charges are overturned.

It's one thing to hear about a person's power, but it's another thing to meet them face to face and witness their genius and intellect up close and personal. I consider Larry Hoover a living legend because of the legendary things he's done. I witnessed the character traits he has which helped him organize people to transform their communities for the better.

We established a bond after the first meeting and began to communicate more. Our level of respect for one another had increased during this meeting of the minds. Our conversations were all about the passion we shared for the streets, and finding ways to make conditions better for our people. Our conversations were so real we didn't want to keep them a secret, so we taped a phone call and used part of it as the intro for the Geto Boys' 1996 album *The Resurrection*. When word got out that I planned to do this, there was great anticipation and excitement in the streets, but also controversy and animosity among law enforcement personnel. I even received threats warning me to not use the audio on the album. I figured that if they could record me visiting Larry without my knowledge or consent, I could record Larry without their permission. That's what gangsters do. We tell the truth, even if no one wants to hear it.

Most people don't like to hear the truth raw and uncut, just like they don't like to take medicine. It may not taste good, but it's good *for* you.

Everyone doesn't have enough respect to be able to speak and reach the hearts of hardcore street guys. But Larry Hoover has that gift. Like he explained on the Geto Boys' album, "See, these young brothas, they pay attention to what I say because I'm one of them. I understand where they been. I come from where they come from. I'm where they going to be if they don't watch what they doing."

So ask yourself, why do the powers that be act like Larry Hoover, the man who has this gift, is dead and doesn't matter? Larry Hoover is alive! They've been keeping him in maximum isolation in solitary confinement since 1997 at the ADMAX in Florence, Colorado, "the Alcatraz of the Rockies."

Currently M.A. Stancil is the warden, but J. Oliver and Charles Daniels were his predecessors. They've been breaking their own laws. They have a Caucasian who doesn't understand our culture or lingo in a position of power, listening to every phone call and spying on every visitation, falsely flagging words as "gangster codes" just to further punish and isolate Larry from simply communicating with his family. Larry has been restricted from even seeing his family for more than six months. According to the prison administrators, his five year old grandson visiting in a Batman costume qualifies as "gang-related."

The warden and his staff have the power to decide who Larry can and cannot speak to or visit, depending on how they feel. They make these decisions without any explanation. They've labeled his family members as security risks and ceased their visitation rights on the spot - Larry's sister, son, grandchildren, and even wife.

I overstand this conspiracy against an intelligent Black man like Larry Hoover, because I've read about Martin Luther King Jr. and Malcolm X. I understand why the enemy is afraid of him and wants to destroy him. Studying the schemes the government used against intelligent Black men who came before me became very useful later when my own life and freedom came under attack. I created a movement with the Geto Boys and inspired others to dream and take action, just like Larry, so I became a target.

I know some people may not understand the depth of these words, and that's okay. It's simple: two wrongs don't make it right. This type of racism can't be accepted in 2018.

GOAL #10

THE ART & SCIENCE OF

respect

ryan Turner started Priority Records in 1985 and had some early success selling compilation CDs of the animated characters *The California Raisins*. It wasn't until Jerry Heller walked in his office with Dr. Dre, Eazy-E, and Ice Cube that Bryan, a white Canadian, got into the rap business. Since then, he'd built his label by taking chances on hardcore rap that no one else would touch. And he took the same chance on me. After my experience with Def American and Warner Bros, I wanted to deal with a label that *wanted* to be in the hardcore rap business, because we weren't going to change our sound or compromise our lyrics for anyone. Bryan had been dealing with N.W.A for years, and he'd also been in the record business a lot longer than I had. We'd been selling gold records, but I wanted to take things to the next level and go platinum.

When I first signed a distribution deal for Rap-A-Lot Records through Priority, they were charging us almost 40%. My partner Cliff had negotiated the deal. At that point, we were still an independent label and hadn't officially sold a million records. You can sell a million records through mom-and-pop record stores, barbershops and the trunk of your cars, but before SoundScan, it was nearly impossible to verify those numbers.

It was the 1990s, and everyone was making money hand over fist, but 40% was still high. I felt that I should've been charged somewhere in the low 20s, especially after the success of "Mind Playing Tricks on Me." The single was our first to reach the Billboard Top 100 chart and was certified gold. The album, *We Can't Be Stopped*, our raw and unapologetic response to the political backlash against us, was the first Rap-A-Lot release to be certified platinum.

The tenth and final goal I'd written down on my list was to renegotiate our distribution deal with Priority. I asked several business associates for advice, and everyone told me the same thing - it was a contract, it was law. It couldn't be undone; it couldn't be broken. No one thought I would be able to change the contract.

My attorney agreed with me that based on the success we were having and the numbers we were selling, 40% was too high. He also represented Bryan at Priority, so he reached out to him and asked him to renegotiate the deal. Bryan acknowledged that if we had been selling those numbers prior to Cliff negotiating the original Rap-A-Lot deal, the distribution fee would be much lower. However, even after acknowledging that, he still refused to compromise or give me any relief by renegotiating a lower distribution fee, and that wasn't good business. My attorney told me that the contract couldn't be changed, and we'd just have to deal with it.

They were playing hardball, and that didn't sit well with me. Bryan Turner was abusing his power by taking nearly half of what we were earning. I wasn't going to "deal with" anything. My early career in the music business was all trial and error. I often felt like I was lacing up my Nikes to run a race where all my opponents were sitting on Harley Davidsons.

Eventually I decided to take some advice from *Think and Grow Rich* and focus on my strengths to get the deal renegotiated. And my strengths were in the streets. So I reached out to some associates and asked them to do a little legwork.

My company was being squeezed, which meant my family was being squeezed. And that made me uncomfortable. So my objective was to make Bryan Turner uncomfortable.

Bryan had stopped returning my phone calls. After a few weeks of surveillance and investigation, I made another call to Bryan's office.

Assistant: Priority Records. May I help you?
James Prince: Yeah, this is James Prince. I would like to speak with Bryan Turner.
(HOLD)
Assistant: James, Bryan is not in the office at the moment. May I take a message?
James: Yeah. Tell Bryan to come to the phone with the red sweater and those blue jeans on. The ones that he's wearing right now.
(HOLD)
Bryan: Hey James! How are you? You in town? Are you here? Are you here?

James: No. I'm not in town. But uh, I have something I want to say to you. I want you to hear me out, and hear me real clear, 'cause after I say this today it's out of my hands. This is a courtesy call. I have some homies who are really upset with the way you're treating us. They know we've done great business with you and deserve a better fee. But at this point, they are upset and this is out of my hands. They know you live at [address redacted], and a bunch of other stuff. Bottom line is, we want to be released within the hour. I can no longer control these fools.

Fifteen minutes later, a contract releasing us from our deal with Priority came through the fax machine.

I know what you're thinking. How could I threaten a man and his family? Simple. Bryan Turner was threatening me and mine. By taking such an extremely high distribution fee, he was damaging our ability to make money, which affected my ability to put food on my family's table. His family was eating just fine. No one should be able to sleep comfortably at night when they're not doing good business. If your own conscience isn't enough to wake you up, I have no problem doing it for you.

Of course, this was years ago, and time and experience has taught me much more about corporate politics. But if I could go back and talk to myself in 1992, so young and green, I wouldn't tell myself to be nicer with Bryan Turner. I would advise myself not to take such a bum deal in the first place. But you live and you learn. And if you do it right, you make money. Though Bryan didn't like the tactics I used to get out of my contract, at the end of the day, he must have respected me and my business savvy. When I came back to him later with an opportunity, he jumped at the chance.

CHESS NOT CHECKERS (THE GAME IS TO BE SOLD, NOT TOLD)

M y attorney had told me it was impossible, but now that I'd signed our release papers from Priority Records, I was focused on getting a better deal. I flew to Los Angeles to meet with Capitol Records, but my intuition told me it wasn't the right fit for Rap-A-Lot. After Capitol, we had a meeting with Irving Azoff, a longtime head of Warner Bros. He had his own company, Giant Records, which was a subsidiary of Warner Bros.

Irving was shorter than me, talked fast, and could hold three different phone conversations at the same time. He was impressive. The meeting was my opportunity to let him know who I was, and let him know that I'd fight for my rights. If you don't speak their lingo from a position of strength, they will run all over you. But when you do talk that talk and walk that walk, they have no choice but to give you the respect you deserve.

If I had settled with the original Priority contract, I would have missed out on some of the most lucrative years of my career. I knew I had to fight, and I had to fight without my attorney, because he sided with Bryan at Priority. When you know you're right, you've gotta keep swinging, even if you've gotta do it alone. Whatever you do, never stop swinging.

My strategy was to use my meeting with Capitol as leverage to spark interest from Warner Bros. Warner Bros was already home to West Coast rapper Ice-T, so they knew how to market hardcore rap. I felt it was a better fit for us. But Irving was already one step ahead of me. The moment I began talking about Capitol, he jumped in and told me everything that was said in the very meeting I'd just left. This motherfucker knew everyone.

I had to shift my negotiation strategy. Since he knew everyone, I used that to my advantage and started to mention all of the people we had in common. The meeting was a success; within a matter of days we drew up a contract for Rap-A-Lot to come aboard the Warner Bros family. I remember thinking what a crazy few weeks it had been; it had only been a few weeks since we'd first asked Bryan to renegotiate.

After we signed the contract for the Warner Bros deal, I went out to my ranch to clear my mind and wait for the money to hit our accounts. And that's when I got a call from Irving - there was a problem. Warner Bros had been catching a lot of heat from Ice-T's new song "Cop Killer," and the board had blocked the deal. As a publicly traded company, they had shareholders to worry about, and the last thing they wanted was to get in bed with an entirely new group of gangster rappers. Irving knew that we'd already fought Def American and Geffen, and even though we were excited to work with Warner Bros, toning down our lyrics wasn't even an option. The deal was off. I was without a distributor in the eleventh hour. I had to think fast.

This time when I called, Bryan Turner at Priority answered the phone right away. He knew he hadn't been fair in our past business dealings. But now he also knew what happens when you back me into a corner. My survival instincts kicked in. That was the Fifth Ward in me. Let the chess game begin. I told Bryan that I was about to sign a new deal with Warner Bros, but as a courtesy, I was offering him one chance to beat their offer.

Here's the number one rule in business: success changes everything. Bryan made a lot of money with Rap-A-Lot Records, which put us in a position to be able to go back to him. If we'd just been a middle-of-the-road company, there's no way he would've taken my call again. That's why it's important to always be successful. Success isn't just about income; success is also about having options. Priority Records was still an option, but Bryan Turner had to work fast. Warner Bros was offering me a distribution fee in the low 20s, and if Bryan wanted us back, he had to beat their offer. I even faxed him over a copy of the agreement. It didn't matter that Warner Bros had already passed. This was like a high-stake poker game, and my poker face was real.

I got off the phone with Bryan and walked out into the field behind my ranch. At night it's nothing but darkness for miles and miles. When you're out there by yourself, you get a feeling of being both incredibly alone and connected to everything at the same time. It's where I feel

God. I looked up at the bright stars and I closed my eyes and just said thank you. I was thanking God for the victory in advance. I knew that no matter what, I'd left it all on the field. I played my hand the best I could and now the rest was up to God.

An hour later a fax came through. Bryan was offering 18%. We went back and forth over the next few hours, negotiating the manufacturing costs, payment turnaround, and a few other details. I negotiated manufacturing costs because I've learned that raising the manufacturing is a method that majors use to offset lowering the distribution percentage. So you might think you're getting a lower distribution fee, but in reality, you're paying for it with a higher manufacturing cost. This time around, I was seasoned, and I knew how to get exactly what I wanted. We signed the deal the following day. Rap-A-Lot was back with Priority and we continued successfully for another three years.

Now that I had accomplished the tenth goal, my next focus was becoming a millionaire outside of Rap-A-Lot. I was beginning to see that while I didn't have the same business background as my peers, there were invaluable skills I possessed that could've only come from the streets.

BIG PICTURE THINKING

THE ART & SCIENCE OF respect

Houston's unemployment rates in the 1990s were as high as 5.8%, but it was nearly double that in the Fifth Ward. The University of Texas, Memorial Herman Healthcare, and Continental Airlines were a few of the largest employers, but if you didn't have a college degree, or if you had a criminal record, you'd be better off hustling. I decided early on that those were the people I wanted to hire, the ones who were living in the margins. These are the people who are often overlooked because they aren't qualified or in the right position to get opportunities to better their lives. I was one of these people, and I got out, so I made it my duty to help as many others as I could.

I filled the Rap-A-Lot offices with ex-convicts, high school dropouts, former drug dealers, and recovering drug addicts. A few people had college degrees, but most of the staff were people who had been turned down everywhere else. Together we built the number one independent record label in the United States. It wasn't long before other labels came along, trying to poach my best employees, offering to double their salaries. But for most of them, it wasn't about the money. It was about loyalty.

Mike Mack, for example, was a guy I'd known for years. He started off part-time with Rap-A-Lot, making $150 a week. He eventually worked his way up to a full-time position, where he was in charge of street promotion. This was 1993, and the record business was booming. There was money to be made, but you had to be smart and aware of your competition at all times.

One day Mike came to me and said that Virgin Records had approached him. They saw his value and offered him $100,000 a year to jump ship and come work for them. He wanted me to know that he was loyal to me and said he'd only take the job with my blessings. I told him I needed to sleep on it. The next day I told him to take the job, but I wanted him to be my eyes and ears inside of Virgin. Throughout my entire career in the music business, I'd been an outsider, an independent. I'd been dealing with the big labels as distributors for years, but here was an opportunity to learn from the inside. I was always curious how the major labels did things, and now thanks to Mike, I was going to find out.

One morning, late in 1993, I was reading *Billboard* and saw something interesting. It listed Rap-A-Lot as the #1 Independent Record Label, and Virgin as the #1 Major Record Label. The next morning, I called Mike and asked who was the head guy at Virgin. I wasn't talking about his direct supervisor, I wanted to know who was really running the show over there. Mike told me it was a guy named Ken Berry, a Brit who co-founded Virgin with Sir Richard Branson. I told Mike I wanted to speak directly to Ken, not a middleman, and he was able to arrange a call that afternoon.

"Congratulations on being the #1 major record label!" I told Ken. "We happen to be the #1 independent label." I told him I thought it would be great if the two top labels in the country did some business together. I was nearing the end of my distribution deal with Priority and was looking for other options. Ken laughed and said he liked the sound of that, but explained that he was leaving for London that night to meet with The Rolling Stones. I said, "Why don't you cancel The Rolling Stones and come meet with me?" and we both laughed.

Ken told me in his British accent, "You know what, James? I think you may be right. Let me see if I can shift some things around."

Ken flew to Houston that night, and we met at the Four Seasons and talked for a few hours. Then Ken got in my car and rode with me to the Fifth Ward. He was fascinated to see my world and where I came from. Hours passed, and still, in the back of my mind, I'm wondering why this guy would cancel with The Rolling Stones to meet with me.

Finally, when we got back to the hotel, I asked him. "Ken, explain to me why you would cancel a meeting with The Rolling Stones and fly to meet me at the drop of a hat?"

He told me, "In this business, there are really special deals that come across the table once in a lifetime. When these types of deals reveal themselves, you waste no time in closing them." He looked at me and added, "I feel this is one of those special deals."

Immediately, my entrepreneurial sense kicked in, and I knew I was dealing with a serious player. And he sensed there was something special about to happen between Virgin and Rap-A-Lot. We ended up releasing some of our most successful records through their Noo Trybe division and then five years later, we did a deal directly through Virgin.

Major labels were trying to do deals with me all the time after we became successful. Everyone who had turned me down in the beginning started trying to do business with us. When I chose not to be selfish with Mike Mack and let him go to Virgin instead of keeping him at Rap-A-Lot, it felt real, like it was about to evolve into something bigger. If I had held onto Mike Mack out of nothing but pure ego, I might never have connected with Ken. And if I acted timidly, Ken wouldn't have flown to Houston to meet with me. I made the right move at the right time, Ken embraced us, I took control, and we worked out a very lucrative deal. Fortune favors the bold, so never be afraid to stick your neck out on your own behalf.

MURDER INC

Sometime in the late 1990s, I'd been introduced to a producer named Seven Aurelius through Tyrin Turner, an actor best known for his role in *Menace II Society*. At the time, Seven was basically homeless in Los Angeles, but he was very gifted. I signed him to a production and publishing deal and moved him out to Houston to produce all of my artists at Rap-A-Lot.

I had a hard time getting some of the more hardcore artists to work with Seven because they considered him strange. He was a weird guy; very eccentric. He wore a lot of purple; he liked to go in the studio and turn off all the lights and use candles instead.

I had been doing some recording with a woman named Erica, and Seven produced several tracks for her. Erica asked if I would fly her to L.A. to be in a Ja Rule video. I bought her a ticket, and told her that she should play some of her music for Irv Gotti. Erica was an attractive girl, so I felt like Irv would at least give her the respect of listening to her music.

Erica came back and told me that Irv listened to her music, but he seemed more interested in the producer than her voice. If Irv Gotti was asking about Seven, that seemed like an opportunity. So I told her to pass along Seven's number. She arranged things, the two dots connected, and Irv flew Seven to New York. I continued monitoring the situation through Erica, and everything moved quickly. She told me that Seven had already produced nine or ten tracks for Ja Rule, and I'm thinking, *Whoa. Seven ain't told them he's with me?*

After the Ja Rule album was released, I thought about making my presence known and letting them know that I owned his publishing. But then Erica told me that Seven was working with Ashanti. So I decided to just be quiet a little longer while I let the dollars stack up. And they did. Murder Inc even licensed a Scarface song, "Mary Jane," for Ashanti's record "Baby," but still, nobody acknowledged that I was Seven's publisher.

I waited until the show was over and all the songs had came out before I reached out to Irv Gotti, and we spoke for the first time. I said, "Irv, I don't know if anybody had told you, but this boy Seven is with me." Irv was rather surprised. I told him, "Let's do good business. I'm calling to see if you've got a problem with doing good business."

Irv was a scholar and a gentleman about the whole situation. He sent his brother Chris Gotti and Supreme down here to meet with me. Kenneth "Supreme" McGriff is a well-respected guy in the streets of New York. I happened to be at my ranch when they arrived in Houston, and Chris always tells me a funny story about that trip. As they were riding down the long, dark road headed out to the ranch, Chris says Supreme nudged him with his elbow and said, "Man, we going out like this?? This is our last ride??"

It wasn't their last ride. They came to the ranch and we all introduced ourselves and it was a beautiful meeting. Irv had done a deal with Seven and he'd also done a publishing deal with Famous Publishing, so there was a lot of confusion, but eventually we got it all straightened out.

Seven didn't handle things properly, but I went in and rescued him and did right by him as well. He wasn't very business savvy and the deals he'd done with Irv and Famous Publishing weren't good deals. He just wanted to make it, so for him to be in the studio with Ashanti and Ja Rule, who were huge at the time, was a dream come true for him. Since then, Seven has produced for everyone from Mary J. Blige to J. Lo, and I own the publishing on all those songs. So my initial investment of signing him and bringing him out to Houston paid off.

Timing is everything in this game, and the techniques I used here helped make me a lot of money. I saw a golden opportunity. There's a time and a place for everything. I knew that if I revealed my hand too soon, they'd just get another producer. Everybody is in business to maintain control and keep as much of the profits in-house as possible. So if they knew they couldn't own the publishing, they probably would have changed the songs instead of making a bunch of money for someone else. So I finessed the situation - through a female.

Still, it ended up being a lucrative situation for everyone involved, and to this day, I consider Irv, Chris, and Supreme to be friends. The relationship we established eventually led to the idea of me, Irv, and Suge Knight coming together to create our own black-owned distribution company. We all had a meeting at a hotel in Beverly Hills to strategize. The project was so much bigger than any one of us, so I was willing to set aside any of my previous hesitations about doing business with Suge. I do business with a lot of people I don't like. It's just business.

It was an interesting conversation, and when we announced our plans, we got a whole lot of attention from the government. Suge and Death Row were attacked, and we all know how that ended up. The Feds basically ran Murder Inc out of business and tried to take their freedom away. I was attacked by the DEA on another level. It was real coincidental that all those attacks took place right when we were putting our heads together to create a monster. It's almost like they dropped an atomic bomb and my company is the only one that survived. Unfortunately, our idea never came to fruition.

PENNY WISE, DOLLAR DUMB

By 2001, my old friend Lyor Cohen had come a long way from the music manager I'd once met in New York. He was now the head of Warner Bros, and was able to do what Irving Azoff hadn't been able to do for us back in the 1990s. Times had changed in the past decade since Warner Bros refused to be in the hardcore rap business. In fact, by the late 1990s, *everyone* wanted to be in the rap business. Moguls/artists like Sean "Puffy" Combs, Shawn "Jay-Z" Carter, and Percy "Master P" Miller were making more commercially viable music, which helped rap music gain mainstream acceptance. It was great for many of us. But it was also a time that separated the boys from the men.

Lyor was working with Todd Moscowitz on a new label called Asylum Records, which Warner Bros built specifically for rap. Asylum was a good fit for Rap-A-Lot, and I made it clear to Todd that I was on board as long as they met my terms, which included a non-compete clause. Asylum was new to the rap world, so the last thing I wanted was to open the doors to my house and allow them to run away with it. The non-compete clause meant that I would have the first right of refusal to be involved with any deal Asylum would make with anyone from my area. This was important, and came in handy later.

Swisha House was a Houston record label started by Michael "5000" Watts, G Dash, and producer/DJ OG Ron C. Their chopped and screwed mixtapes were big in the South, but it was their hit "Still Tippin'" with Mike Jones in 2004 that put them on the national radar. Asylum was interested, and I was already on the case.

Michael Watts and I met, and I put it straight to him: it was in the best interest of Swisha House to do a partnership deal with Rap-A-Lot and be distributed by Asylum. This meant that we would do a 50/50 joint venture deal. I would put up all the money for Swisha House's production, marketing, and promotion, and Asylum would simply distribute the records. It was a good deal for them because I would be assuming 100% of the risk. In short, I was taking them in as Rap-A-Lot family. Mike told me that sounded good, so Todd and I started working on the paperwork.

After a few weeks, we hit a snag. Todd came back and told me that Swisha House wanted to do the deal with Asylum, but didn't want me involved. So I didn't fight them. Instead of the partnership agreement, Asylum and I did a 50/50 split and gave Swisha House a production deal.

All of my career I've been passionate about artists from the South, so I fought for them. I knew they would follow my lead, so I secured my paperwork. My company was lucrative, and Asylum knew that others would want to do a deal with them after they saw me at the table. Even though the deal I offered Swisha House was better, they chose to go with a bigger company for less.

Swisha House's first two releases through Asylum went platinum, and everyone was happy until the royalty checks arrived. Swisha House received a small cut, while Rap-A-Lot and Asylum split the bulk of the revenue down the middle. G Dash circled back around, asking if we could revisit the partnership conversation. He admitted they made a grave mistake by not taking the offer the first time. I understood where they were coming from, however, ignorance is one thing. Picking the wrong horse is another. I told them if Asylum wanted to cut them in on their 50% that was fine. (I'm sure they didn't.) But my 50% was for the Rap-A-Lot family.

PIMP C & MASTER P

THE ART & SCIENCE OF respect

Every Thursday night, for many years, I played basketball with a group of local guys in Fifth Ward. Just about anyone's invited to play as long as you come correct. It's one of my ways of staying connected to the youth and the streets, making myself accessible to the younger cats coming up, and it's a good way to get a work out.

It was during one of these Thursday night games back in 1999 when I got a phone call from Pimp C. I had met him seven years earlier. It was 1992 when I first heard the record "Pocket Full of Stones," and I'd just bought a brand new Lexus coupe. I almost burned the motor out driving to Port Arthur, Texas, to meet the rappers behind the song. I liked Pimp C right away. He was very upfront. We hung out for several hours, and towards the end of our meeting, Pimp's partner Bun B came by. He was another stand-up guy, smart and respectful. Together they were the duo UGK. I wanted to work with them at that time, but they were already signed to Big Tyme Recordz, who had just done a deal with them through Jive. It was all love regardless, and I left them with my number.

Over the years, both Pimp C and Bun B kept in touch. Just because they weren't signed to me didn't mean I couldn't help with advice or contacts. It's not very often that I like both the music and the artist behind it, so I wanted to see these guys win. But that night in 1999, Pimp C had a bit of a run in with a friend of mine, Percy Miller.

Percy, or "Master P" as he's known all over the world, is a media mogul, platinum-selling rapper, and businessman from New Orleans. His No Limit movement helped do for Louisiana what Rap-A-Lot did for Texas. Although my movement began as a way to help Houston, I always considered the rest of the South to be extended family. When I saw the movement happening in New Orleans with No Limit and Cash Money, I always looked at these young moguls coming up under me as the next generation, adding links in the chain I created. Over the years I'd check in on them, answer the phone when they needed advice, and even send talent their way. It wasn't just about Rap-A-Lot. My God-given purpose was way bigger, and I accepted the responsibilities that came along with that. To this day I consider Master P to be a friend. He's a good guy who never abused his power. Still, some situations call for different solutions.

The dispute between Master P and Pimp C was about respect. Pimp C had always been very vocal, and he felt that Master P owed him some money over the song "Break 'Em Off Something." These kinds of disputes happen all the time when you're dealing with large amounts of money and the type of people we deal with. There's almost always discrepancy between what someone thinks they should be paid and what they're actually owed, and sometimes they're not actually owed anything at all. Either way, Pimp was unhappy about it and made his feelings known during a few shows, and Master P didn't take too kindly to that.

I got a 911 call during my basketball game that Pimp C needed to talk to me, immediately. He had a confrontation with Master P and things had gotten ugly. Music and business aside, we're all just people, and no one likes to feel disrespected, period. Master P felt that the way Pimp C was throwing his name around was disrespectful. Pimp C felt like his pockets were being disrespected. Something had to give. So Pimp C called me. I've been in both situations, and I understood how they both felt, as a label owner and as a man. But Pimp C wanted to be down with Rap-A-Lot.

I'd wanted to do business with Pimp C since the moment I first heard him on a record, so even though this was an inconvenient time, it was the right time. Now he was family, and no one can touch my family without consequences. I got on the phone with Master P and assured him of two things: first, since Pimp C was a part of the Rap-A-Lot family, his disrespectful talk toward P was going to stop. That's not how we do business. We don't run our mouth just for the sake of it. Second, Master P was going have to show respect where respect is due, so he and I could remain on one accord and let sleeping dogs lie. And to Master P's credit, he did. To Pimp C's credit, he didn't say anything else about Master P.

Before we could complete Pimp C's paperwork to join the Rap-A-Lot family as a solo artist, he was sentenced to eight years in prison for a probation violation. This came at difficult time for Bun B, who – like every other artist – needed to record and release music to feed his family. UGK was still signed to Jive Records and owed them one final album. With Pimp C behind bars, that album was on hold indefinitely. But that shouldn't mean Bun B couldn't make a living for him and his family.

Barry Weiss was resistant to the idea of Bun B recording a solo album for another label at first. As the head of Jive Records at the time, his responsibility was to his label, and it was a risk he didn't want to take. We spoke several times by phone, and when it became clear we were getting nowhere, our lawyers got involved. No artist should be put in a position where they can't eat because of red tape. That's not business, that's cruelty. I fought for them.

By using a litigation attorney and effective communication, I was able to make Barry understand that he wouldn't be getting a future UGK album without allowing Pimp C and Bun B to have the freedom of their solo careers. Since Barry was a wise man, both Pimp C and Bun B were allowed to sign with Rap-A-Lot as solo artists, with the under-standing that they'd fulfill their obligations to Jive once Pimp C was released from prison.

We made great music with both Bun B and Pimp C, and I got to work with two guys I loved and respected. Out of all the deals I've done, this was one of the hardest. It took a lot of maneuvering to finally bring it to fruition, and I was happy to be able to help. And after Pimp C came home, Barry was able to release one of the best UGK albums on Jive, *Underground Kingz*.

EAST vs. WEST

I t was November 1994 when Tupac arrived at Manhattan's Quad Studios to record a guest verse. It was in the middle of what I imagine was a stressful time for him; he was on trial for sexual assault. By Pac's own account, he and his group were waiting in the lobby for the elevator when someone approached, demanding all of his jewelry. Tupac was shot five times, twice in the head. He willed himself onto the elevator, up to the studio where Sean "Puffy" Combs, Andre Harrell, and others were present for a Notorious B.I.G. recording session. Tupac later recounted to *VIBE* Magazine what happened next:

"Nobody approached me. I noticed that nobody would look at me. Andre Harrell wouldn't look at me. I had been going to dinner with him the last few days. He had invited me to the set of New York Undercover, *telling me he was going to get me a job. Puffy was standing back too. I knew Puffy. He knew how much stuff I had done for Biggie before he came out."*

Tupac never openly blamed Puffy and Biggie for the shooting, but he had insinuated it often enough in interviews and songs that the public got the idea that they were involved.

Less than two years later, in September 1996, Tupac was shot again, this time in Las Vegas. He sustained six gunshot wounds and died in the hospital six days later.

This was the height of the East Coast and West Coast rivalry. The tension began in the streets, spilled over into songs, and now it had returned to the streets and taken the life of one of rap's biggest stars.

I'd seen Tupac less than a month earlier in Los Angeles. He'd wanted me to come out with him that night. "You gotta come kick it with me!" he kept saying. My father had just come home from jail and I wanted to get back to Houston to see him. No more than three weeks later, Pac was gone. It was an unfortunate situation. Still, I remained neutral.

Being from the South, I had love for both the East Coast and the West Coast. We weren't involved in the back and forth, mainly because it was a distraction which cost more money than it made. Clearly, we were doing what we were doing in the South and they were loving it. We had an influence on both the East and the West. "Not from Houston but I Rap-A-Lot," Biggie rhymed on Craig Mack's "Flava in Ya Ear" remix.

At the time, mainstream media still wasn't taking the South seriously, and they were the driving force in the tension. How the media handled the rivalry had a lot to do with its outcome. It was a street level situation, and many media outlets never understood the streets.

Reporting the news is a fact-based exercise: who, what, when, where and why. But the streets aren't black and white. Despite the many iron-clad codes, the streets function off of one element that the media can't understand: circumstance. No one thinks twice if you stole a car, unless it's the wrong person's car. The streets are a population of people constantly shown by the rest of society that they must fend for themselves. In many ways we're isolated, shut off from opportunities to properly educate ourselves and better our situations. So how can the media accurately report on something happening in the streets? They can't. The media thrives on logic. But the streets are too desperate for logic. To us, context is everything.

A few months after Tupac was killed, in February 1997, we were ready-ing the release of *The Untouchable*, which would become Scarface's most successful album. Face was on a streak and required a lot of cross-country promotion. I was passing through Los Angeles on my tour bus when I got a call informing me that Biggie and Puffy were also in the city filming the music video for "Hypnotize." I rerouted my bus and went to pay Puffy a visit because I had questions and concerns.

Hip Hop was born in, and will always belong first, to the hood. There's a natural relationship that no amount of corporate sanitization can erase. Even if an artist is not from the streets, it's likely that their man-agers, A&Rs, DJ, or homies are, which can help keep the artist in touch with the people. But sometimes those same people can be the biggest threat. That's why there are different types of security for different sit-uations. Rappers move throughout the country with the help of local connections on the ground who are plugged into the streets and can give the artists a lay of the land. These are usually gang members and hustlers who have ties to the record industry but are also respected in their city. These guys are the ones who will tell you what's going down in every hood. Is there beef you need to know about? Which areas you should stay away from. And if those areas can't be avoided, these are the guys who will clear a path for you to make it in and out of the city safely. We're talking about guys with hard-earned reputations. Their name is their bond, and their involvement can mean the difference between a successful trip and a disaster.

"Why are you out here loose in Los Angeles like this?" I asked Puffy. That was the first thing out of my mouth. "It's not safe here for you," I told him. I knew this, just as anyone with their ears to the street knew. Tupac had just been murdered, and even though he was originally from the East, the West had accepted him as one of their own. Bad Boy was in enemy territory. If Puffy was going to be in L.A., he needed better security, and guys who were equipped to handle the kind of heat they were under. I don't think Puffy felt their lives were in danger, or else they wouldn't have been there. But I felt like it was a disaster waiting to happen. If the streets don't want you in their city, don't go.

When I finished talking to Puffy about my concerns, I walked over to Biggie's trailer to speak to him. Although I didn't have a direct stake in this conflict, as a man, I didn't want to see any more bloodshed. Biggie assured me that wouldn't be the case. "It's about the video," Biggie told me. "That's it."

That was the last time I saw the Notorious B.I.G. alive. A month later, he returned to Los Angeles to attend the Soul Train Music Awards. He was shot and killed at the corner of Wilshire and South Fairfax, riding in the passenger seat of his SUV. I was back in Texas when I got the call. It was a tragedy, but unfortunately, I wasn't surprised.

Less than two weeks after Biggie's murder, I was contacted by an investigator who wanted to question me about the conversations I'd had with Puffy and Biggie. "I don't talk to police," was the only thing I had to say. I told him if he wanted to charge me in connection, then charge me. But I knew I'd done nothing wrong. The only thing I was guilty of was trying to warn Puffy and Biggie of the obvious danger. It was none of his business; I didn't need to tell the investigator that. The streets don't talk to police because the police don't work for the hood. They claim their job description is to "protect and serve," but the reality is, that doesn't include impoverished people. It's the same with the media. If something goes wrong, it's our fault. So, I'm not going to help you blame me. Of course, they quickly realized that I wasn't involved and dropped my name from the investigation.

A few months later I got a call from Jimmy Henchman. Now that B.I.G. was gone, the East Coast vs. West Coast rivalry had reached an all-time high. Anyone could be next, and Puffy wanted to meet with me.

Jimmy and Puffy both flew to Houston and expressed their desire for a truce. Two of Hip Hop's biggest stars had been murdered, so I understood the urgency. But why come to me? I was told that it was because I had remained neutral, and was one of very few who had the respect of Suge Knight.

My connection to Suge Knight had come through Harry-O, someone

I've known from my street days. At first, Harry-O couldn't understand why I'd walked away from the game to get into music. He called me one day from the penitentiary where he was serving a life sentence. He needed a new hustle. The producer Dr. Dre was the hottest thing coming out of the West Coast, so I asked Harry-O if he still had any juice on the streets. If you treat the streets right, your name will always hold weight – even from behind bars.

I told Harry-O to get Dr. Dre, the type of genius he needed to build his new company around. The next time I spoke to Harry-O, he'd partnered with an ex-football player, Marion "Suge" Knight, to form a record label. Suge was from Compton, and his reputation preceded him as a man willing to do anything to get results.

When I ended up on a phone call with Suge and Harry-O, I saw immediately that Suge could become a potential problem. Harry-O was calling us on a recorded line from the penitentiary. Anyone who's ever received a call from an inmate knows that as soon as it connects, an automated voice informs you that the call is being recorded. That is your one and only warning to watch your mouth. Still, throughout this call, Suge spoke recklessly about the type of things you don't want the federal government to know about. I said nothing.

When the call was over I thought to myself, *either Suge isn't very bright, or he doesn't care.* Either way, I was uncomfortable. I voiced my concern to Harry-O, who said he'd talk to Suge. Still, on the next call, Suge began to speak recklessly again. This clown was a time bomb waiting to happen. This time I hung up. Harry-O called me back, and I made it very clear to him - and to any members of law enforcement who might be listening - that I had no part in what Suge was talking about. I told him I wouldn't be a part of their Death Row venture, but I'd be happy to cheer them on from the sidelines.

Of course, Death Row went on to sign Dr. Dre after Suge maneuvered him away from his deal with Eazy-E's Ruthless Records. Eventually Snoop Dogg and many others became a part of Death Row. When Pac needed $1.4 million to bond out of jail, Suge was there, and was able to sign him to Death Row. Truthfully, I was about a week away from going to meet with Pac myself to discuss a business deal. But Suge beat me to it.

During the two years that Tupac was a part of Death Row, there had been nothing but music and controversy. Suge, who had been driving the car when Tupac was fatally shot, walked away with only minor injuries. Still, he'd lost his artist and a great investment, and Suge was not the type of man to take that lightly.

Despite all the things that happened, Suge and I were cool. He always showed respect, so he always got respect.

So when Puffy and Jimmy Henchman came to Houston, they wanted me to mediate a truce between Puffy and Suge. They hoped this would effectively end the East Coast and West Coast rivalry. But I had some important questions to ask first: "When Tupac was shot at Quad Studios, did you go to the hospital to check on him? Did you use any of your resources to try to find out who did it?"

Puffy was asking for a truce because he never wanted a war. He said he never had a problem with Tupac, and hated that it had escalated as far as it did. Puffy's an intelligent businessman, but this situation required a lot of street savvy. Most people wouldn't have known what to do. Puff is an artist and a producer, but the streets run deep. When you're a leader in the street game, it can be difficult to find the proper way to lead and protect your team.

After I analyzed how everything was being handled, I realized that I wasn't comfortable being in the middle of Suge and Puffy. I couldn't stand in the middle of bullshit and make it smell good. I hadn't heard anything solid in response to my questions, and I couldn't stand in a weak position with my credibility on the line. I also heard that some people believed Jimmy Henchman had conspired with Puffy and Haitian Jack to shoot Tupac at Quad Studios. There were too many hidden hands, and after I peeped what was happening, I just couldn't be involved in this fight. I didn't feel comfortable in my spirit conducting this meeting.

I chose not to mediate a truce between Puffy and Suge. In order to be a mediator, I needed to understand both sides, and I couldn't say that I did. While I sympathized with Puff's situation, there was so much bad information circulating that no one really knew what to believe. I didn't want to risk getting tangled up in the middle of a truce where I didn't know for certain that I had all the facts. Some things are just a matter of principle.

DR. DRE WENT MISSING

In 2013, Scarface did an interview with *Complex* listing the 25 Most Essential Songs in his catalog. One of those songs was "Game Over" from the 1997 album *The Untouchable,* featuring Ice Cube and Too $hort, and produced by Dr. Dre. Scarface recalled of the record:

"I begged Dr. Dre for the record. I was persistent about getting a record from him. He invited me over to the studio and he did like three or four beats for me. A lot of people say what they want to say about Dre like he don't do his own shit but that's a lie, Dre was hands on. We were very adamant about getting that record from Dre... When we finally got the record, we had trouble clearing it. Jimmy Iovine would not clear [the] record for some reason. Somehow, Dre had a conversation with people over at Interscope and I ended up getting that record for free. I don't know what was said or what was done, all I know is I got to use that record and I never heard anything else about it. At that time a Dre beat was like $75,000 or $100,000."

Well, Dr. Dre doesn't give beats away. Jimmy Iovine does. And even then, it's not for free. Let me explain.

While we were working on that album, Scarface and I were both adamant about getting a Dr. Dre beat. I've been a fan of Dre's since the beginning. The man is a genius. We finally got Scarface in the studio with him to work on some music. Once they settled on a track, the vibe was so West Coast that it only made sense to add some California artists, and Ice Cube and Too $hort jumped on right away. Within weeks we had all three verses. The only thing we needed was a hook. Dre said he'd finish the song and throw a hook on it, pretty much guaranteeing we'd have a banger on our hands. Then, Dr. Dre went missing.

Weeks went by and no one could get Dre on the phone. Finally, Ice Cube did the hook and we finished it ourselves. I pressed up 500,000 copies and we were preparing to ship out when we received a cease and desist letter from Interscope's Jimmy Iovine.

I had some homies in the streets trying to catch up with Dre, to try to get him to talk to Jimmy Iovine and convince him to call off the cease and desist. But the homies didn't have any better luck finding Dre than I did. They'd gone by the studios, his hangout spots, even his house. But when a real street dude doesn't want to be found, he won't be.

This problem required a different solution. Pressing up 500,000 units isn't cheap; that's a major investment. Virgin Records was looking at me cross-eyed, wanting to know why they were legally being prohibited from getting a return on our investment. This was a serious situation.

I reached out to Jimmy Iovine directly, but his secretary told me, "Mr. Iovine is away in the mountains." *The mountains?* That didn't sound right. Some of the homies went up to Jimmy's office and walked right past his secretaries to see him, but he wasn't there.

Out of respect, Jimmy cut his trip short and came home from the mountains early to have a meeting with me. Once we were able to talk and clear things up, it turned out to be nothing but a simple misunderstanding. Jimmy cleared the song and dropped the cease and desist. The use of the song, minus Dre's fee, was a show of good faith on Jimmy's part. I think I ran into Dr. Dre a few years later, but we never discussed the song or his random disappearance.

UNITED STATES OF AMERICA vs. JAMES PRINCE

In 1988, a Chevrolet El Camino was stopped near El Paso, Texas, with dealer paper tags registered to Smith Auto Sales. The driver was my lifelong friend and the passenger was my cousin, but neither of them worked at my dealership. During a routine search of the vehicle, police discovered a hidden compartment which contained 76 kilograms of cocaine. The estimated street value of the cocaine was roughly $4.5 million. Both men were arrested. My cousin, a standout football player headed to college at the University of Houston, remained in jail until his lawyer was able to prove that he had simply caught a ride in the wrong car that night. My friend, the driver, went to trial and was found guilty of felony conspiracy and possession with intent to distribute.

At the time of their arrest, I was about a hundred miles away in the studio on Shepherd & 19th Street, cutting a record. This is when I was splitting my time between the studio and promoting my artists. I'd left the streets alone and was focused on Rap-A-Lot. The car lot, once my headquarters, had become a side venture that made enough money to keep the lights on and the bills paid while I worked to make Rap-A-Lot a success. It was studio all night, sleep in the morning, promotion for the rest of the day, and repeat. What I *wasn't* doing was moving 76 kilos of cocaine.

Federal authorities thought differently. They began a drug investigation on my associates, Smith Auto Sales, and myself. Choices made by a few individuals set the wheels in motion that would affect many people for years to come. Remember what I said earlier about the shepherd carrying the risk for the sheep? The federal government was so determined to connect me to the 76 kilos that on more than one occasion they offered to suspend my friend's lengthy sentence if he would find a way to tie me in, even if it wasn't true. A lesser man would've taken the deal. But my lifelong friend is not a snitch, and he refused to lie on me. He served 18 years of a 21-year sentence.

By 1999, I had been arrested five different times on drug charges, despite the fact that – aside from that one hit off a joint in the fourth grade – I've never done drugs and I wasn't selling drugs. All of those charges were eventually dismissed. One of those incidents occurred in 1993. Late one night, I was headed to a party on Richmond Drive in Houston. I was alone in my Lexus coupe with RAP-A-LOT on the license plates when an officer pulled me over. He approached my window with his gun already drawn and told me to get out of the car. I asked if I was being arrested.

"No, you're not being arrested," he told me, as he put me in the back of his squad car. He started questioning me about how I had beat a previous case. But I wasn't going to talk about a previous case, especially not in the back of a squad car. He still had his gun drawn on me, and told me I was known to be violent. He closed the door, walked out of earshot, and made some phone calls. A short time later two more squad cars arrived and they moved the entire caravan from busy Richmond Drive to a secluded side street. By now, I'd been detained in the back seat of the squad card for almost an hour.

I'd been driving alone when they pulled me over. Now I was separated from my mobile phone, and no one but the officers present even knew I was there. Then they moved me from the first car to the backseat of a different car, where two rookie cops were watching me. I kept asking if I was under arrest, and if so, why not just take me down to the station?

"He's talking to a District Attorney," one of the rookies told me. Finally, the officer who had originally pulled me over walked over to the first squad car and said, "Look what we have here…" He pulled up a little white pill that I'd never seen before. Even until this day, I couldn't identify it. But they were trying to say it was mine. They alleged that it fell out of my pocket in the backseat of the first squad car. They took me down to the local police station, but the commanding officers wouldn't take me, and waved me on to the headquarters. A line of officers were waiting there at the headquarters to taunt me. They said they'd finally gotten me; they said I "just couldn't leave that dope alone." I spent the night in jail.

As I sat there waiting for morning to come, all I could think about was fighting. And I don't mean my fellow inmates. You see, I've always viewed incarcerated people differently. I see people behind bars as just people, separated from society either by bad choices or crooked cops. Throughout the years, I've donated lots of my own money to inmates all over the country. Some are friends; some are even artists who wrote to me, sharing their story, their struggle, because they knew I'd understand. So sitting on a bench in lock-up wasn't my concern. I knew that my real fight would begin the moment I was released the following morning.

I made bail and went directly to the hospital, where I was drug-tested. Then my attorney arranged for me to take a polygraph. I made the results of both of these tests public to show everyone that I had nothing to hide. Two busloads of homies from the hood showed up in front of the police station to protest my unlawful arrest.

Meanwhile, that one little pill kept changing. At first officers alleged that the pill was ecstasy. Then the pill became Mandrake, also known as a Quaalude, which would make it a felony charge. But even before the first court date the district attorney dropped the charges to a misdemeanor. Now, he claimed that the pill was Valium. He wanted me to accept a plea, but I wasn't going to accept anything. I'd done nothing wrong, and there was no way I was going to allow the D.A. or anyone else to back me into a corner and make me admit to something I know I didn't do. When I didn't accept the plea, they dropped the charges. But I had started a war. Not only did I beat another case, I'd publicly flexed my muscle with the protest. In the eyes of the law, I had become the worst kind of citizen: one they couldn't control. So they turned up the heat. That was in 1993. In the years to follow, it would get much worse. Just about everyone coming out of Rap-A-Lot's compound was stopped. Squad cars or unmarked police cars would camp out on the surrounding corners, waiting to pull over everyone from employees to business associates. Even my attorney was stopped.

The routine was almost always the same. They'd stop the car, pull us out, search it, ask us all kinds of questions, and when they didn't find anything, we were sent on our way. This went on for months. By then I was a pretty wealthy man, having made my money in a number of different ventures including entertainment, real estate, and many others. I was paying hefty sales, income, and property taxes on all of these legitimate businesses, and my hard-earned tax dollars were being used to pay police officers to camp outside of my office daily and harass my employees and myself.

It was around 3 AM one night in January 1999 when Chris Simon, Michael Wortham and Aaron Battle were coming home from Jamaica Jamaica, a Houston nightclub. The three men worked for me as a part of my promotional team, and they'd been riding around in a Rap-A-Lot van, wrapped with images of our artists. A Houston Police Department patrol car followed them from the club and finally pulled them over on a desolate access road several miles later. The three men were taken out of the van, handcuffed and beaten, physically abused and threatened. They were then taken to the DEA field office, where they were stripped, cavity-searched, and interrogated throughout the night. The agents asked questions about me, insisting that I was a "drug-dealing gang lord." The officers even took Chris' gold Rap-A-Lot chain, valued at over $1,200. The men were eventually released the next morning without charges. What the three men were given were death threats to send back to me.

A few months later, it was past 2 AM when I departed my office, driving alone in my Prowler. A Department of Public Safety officer pulled me over on Highway 290 and instructed me to exit on 43rd Street, specifically telling me to turn into the McDonald's parking lot. This was the only time in my life that I've ever been pulled over and instructed to pull over again, several miles away. By now, to protect myself both against potential robberies and harassment from law enforcement, I'd developed a system. I always travel as a part of a caravan to ensure my safety. I still move the same way today. But on this night, law enforcement hadn't figured that out yet. As the officers pulled me over, my team following behind pulled over far enough away as to not interfere or be seen, but close enough to remain within reach if I needed them.

I followed the officer's instructions and exited Highway 290 at 43rd Street. But as I exited the ramp, I noticed that the McDonald's was closed. Not only was it closed, but all the lights in the parking lot were off. They wanted me to pull into a big blind spot. I was on the phone with a member of my team who was riding in one of the two cars behind me. He agreed that it was a bad idea. I told him to keep circling the area, and I pulled into the Shell gas station parking lot across the street instead. The officer followed behind me. He came up to the car yelling, "Didn't I tell you to pull into the McDonald's? Why didn't you do as you were told?"

"Sir, I didn't want you to think I was trying to harm you in that dark parking lot," I responded. "And I didn't want to think that you were trying to harm me."

Then I asked, "What's the problem?" He didn't have an answer. He told me he'd pulled me over because I was swerving. I don't smoke or drink, so there was no way I was swerving. Then he asked me, "Where are your guns, Mr. Prince?" He hadn't yet asked me for my license or registration, but he already knew my name. I told him my guns were under my floor mat, and he told me to get out of the car. Concealed weapons are legal in Texas, and I believe in exercising my right to bear arms. But as I watched the officer kneel in my car, he was searching everywhere *except* where my guns were kept.

"Hey man, what you doing?" I asked him. "You're violating my rights!" My brand new Prowler at the Shell station with an officer searching inside was starting to cause a bit of a scene. Now, not only were my two homies watching, but a few additional cars pulled up. Clearly, the officer's plan wasn't going as he'd hoped.

Finally, I saw a Cutlass slowly ride out of the darkness of the McDonald's parking lot and pull alongside the DPS car. A white man in his 30s got out, dressed in full tactical gear, including a bulletproof vest and eye black on his face. Eye black is the black paint someone wears under their eyes. It's purpose is to cut glare from sunlight or any other light that might distract from your target. It's worn by athletes, military personnel in combat, and hunters.

The man from the Cutlass walked over to the DPS car and spoke with the officer in a low, hushed tone. They looked over at me a few times, and then the man got back in his car and rode off. I didn't know what to make of it. It wasn't a farfetched idea that someone trying to rob me would hire a DPS officer to lure me off the highway, but that's a ballsy move. I was already in my car when the DPS officer came back to tell me he was letting me go with a warning. But I knew he wasn't the real problem. I was concerned about the guy in the Cutlass. Whoever he worked for was out to get me, and I probably wouldn't survive it.

My lawyer suggested we hire a private investigator, P.M. Clinton, who came highly recommended. His assignment was to find out more about the people investigating me. Things had quickly escalated from police harassment to a credible attempt on my life, and I had a right to know why. But even Clinton wasn't prepared for what he would find.

The private investigator learned that the man dressed in tactical gear in the Cutlass was a DEA agent named Chad Scott. He and another DEA agent named Jack Schumacher had been handpicked to lead the investigation into Rap-A-Lot Records and myself. For years, the DEA had been working with the IRS to try to prove that I was a criminal. They thought I was trafficking narcotics or running one of the largest gang networks in the South. The government simply did not believe that I could have built my fortune legally, and they brought in these two very dangerous men to try to prove it.

Agent Jack Schumacher has killed six individuals in the line of duty, almost all of whom were the subject of his investigation. All of them were shot dead while he claimed to be "attempting" to make their arrest. Although his "use of deadly force" was cleared by the respective agencies in each situation, six people dead sounds like more than a coincidence to me. Or maybe there are a lot of dark parking lot conversations at two in the morning.

The private investigator continued to research agent Jack Schumacher by speaking with his former commanding officers and colleagues. They all said the same thing: Jack Schumacher is a dangerous man. Clinton learned first-hand just how dangerous he was when his father-in-law received a phone call out of the blue from agent Jack Schumacher, asking to play golf with Investigator Clinton's son. For a moment, Clinton considered letting his son – then in his early 20s – accept the golf invitation. Jack Schumacher even made reservations at the club where Clinton's son was a member. But when friends of Jack Schumacher advised against it, Clinton realized the type of individual he was dealing with and decided not to put his son in any more danger.

Clinton's final report on Jack Schumacher gave me enough information to realize that in order to protect my own life and the lives of my family and employees, I would have to get political.

THE ART & SCIENCE OF WAR

No one sends you a letter informing you that you're being investigated by the DEA. There's no formal announcement in the press or even a courtesy call to let you know that representatives of the local, state and federal government are combing through your life, looking for any minute thing that could possibly be interpreted as a tie to wrongdoing. You just start getting harassed.

My friends and I had experienced racial profiling growing up in the hood for so long that we damn near were immune to it. As a black man from the hood, I know what to expect when I'm riding around in a car that costs more than some homes. I know I'm going to get pulled over. The long-standing debate over whether it's okay for law enforcement to stop minorities more frequently than whites isn't my point here. When law enforcement agencies are already investigating you, they'll give you any reason for pulling you over just to have a reason to write on their form.

The real reason you're being unlawfully detained is so they can mess with you. They want to disrupt your life. They think that their interruptions of your daily tax-paying life will cause a shift in your routine, revealing whichever criminal activity they suspect you're involved with. But if you're not guilty of anything, it's just plain old harassment.

Again, I'd witnessed racial profiling all my life, even as a child, before I became a recipient of it. I saw my friends being pulled over and harassed. I witnessed drugs being planted on them. I witnessed them being set up. Then I became a victim of the very same things. But I was able to get my cases dismissed because I had the will to fight, and the wisdom and the funds to get the right people to fight with me. During those fights, I was not only telling the truth about my situation, but also took the opportunity to shine the spotlight and expose the corruption and lawlessness in these federal, state, and local agencies.

The benefit of having a record label is that it gives you a platform. Just like law enforcement agencies have the ability to bottleneck a street for a checkpoint, or release information on crimes, criminals or public safety concerns, I have the ability to do the same thing in other ways.

I've never been one for much talking. I observe my surroundings, keep close counsel, and when I have something to say, I make it quick and clear. And I prefer to put it on record. This is what I've done since I started Rap-A-Lot in 1986, and it's what I continue to do today. By putting it on record, I'm holding everyone to a standard of truth and accountability. It doesn't leave any room for open questions or any doubt about how serious I am.

Law enforcement wants us to believe that they are the ultimate power.

They pledge to serve and protect the people, and they're also being funded by the people. But when one person takes issue with how they are treated by law enforcement, they're often vilified instead of being heard. This is how some police maintain control. Not by listening to the people that they're sworn to serve, but instead by manipulating the weak and vulnerable with bully tactics. And just as I am not a cocaine dealer, I am neither weak nor vulnerable. If you harass me, I will use my platform to tell the entire world about it. This was like fighting Big Carl all over again. And just like back in Dogan Elementary School, I was not going to be intimidated by the size of my adversary. Jack Schumacher and Chad Scott had made what I believe to be an attempt on my life, and I needed to know if they were acting on their own or if the DEA, a part of the United States government, was a part of it.

I know that some of you will find this hard to believe. Depending on where you're from, the idea that a federal agent would make an attempt on the life of a private citizen may strike you as either ridiculous or not at all surprising. But the FBI defines a "serial killer" as "a person responsible for killing two or more people, with a cooling-off period between each death." Agent Jack Schumacher had six kills. I had to take that seriously.

You can't just walk into a DEA field office and report that an officer is trying to kill you. Or at least I wasn't going to. Instead, I reached out to Congresswoman Maxine Waters through a mutual acquaintance. She had built a reputation as a champion for people of color who didn't have a voice. In many ways, I felt like I was being silenced.

It took a few months, but eventually I was able to arrange a meeting with Maxine. Instead of just sitting down in front of her and accusing a DEA agent of making an attempt on my life, I presented my case properly. I first invited her to take a look at my business dealings, and we toured my businesses. Finally, I presented her with Investigator Clinton's findings. Congresswoman Waters agreed to help me.

August 20, 1999
Ms. Janet Reno
Attorney General
U.S. Department of Justice
Constitution Avenue & 10th Street, N.W.
Washington, D.C. 20530

Dear Attorney General Reno,

Pursuant to our telephone conversation this morning, I am writing to request your assistance on what I believe to be an urgent matter. Mr. James Prince, owner of Rap-A-Lot Records, believes his life to be in danger at the hands of rogue officers from the Drug Enforcement Agency (DEA) in Houston, Texas.

James Prince is a 34 year-old, African-American entrepreneur who has created a very successful business producing and managing rap artists. It is my understanding that Mr. Prince has amassed sizable assets from his business which is operating out of Houston, Texas. Mr. Prince believes that he is being harassed and intimidated by the DEA officials in his hometown of Houston because of their assumption regarding the legitimacy of his business finances.

Mr. Prince alleges that the DEA has accused him of earning the profits from his business illegally. In addition, he alleges that he has been subjected to racial slurs,

WATERS

DEPUTY WHIP

AND FINANCIAL
AVICES

JUDICIARY

Congress of the United States
House of Representatives
Washington, DC 20515-0535

Please Reply To
Washington, DC 20515-0535
(202) 225-2201
Fax (202) 225-7854

Los Angeles, CA 90003
(323) 757-8900
Fax (323) 757-9506

August 20, 1999

Ms. Janet F. Reno
Attorney General
U.S. Department of Justice
Constitution Avenue & 10th Street, N.W.
Washington, D.C. 20530

Dear Attorney General Reno·

    Pursuant to our telephone conversation this morning, I am writing to request your assistance on what I believe to be an urgent matter. Mr. James Prince, owner of Rap-A-Lot Records, believes his life to be in danger at the hands of rogue officers from the Drug Enforcement Agency (DEA) in Houston, Texas.

    .James Prince is a 34 year-old, African-American entrepreneur who has created a very successful business producing and managing rap artists. It is my understanding that Mr. Prince has amassed sizeable assets from his business which is operating out of Houston, Texas. Mr. Prince believes that he is being harassed and intimidated by the DEA officials in his hometown of Houston because of their assumption regarding the legitimacy of his business finances.

    Mr. Prince alleges that the DEA has accused him of earning the profits from his business illegally. In addition, he alleges that he has been subjected to racial slurs, the illegal search of his automobile, and that his customers and workers are stopped and questioned without provocation by the DEA. Mr. Prince also has raised concerns about the interference in his right to travel, and he has been stopped numerous times on dark stretches of Texas highways. Simply put, Mr. Prince believes strongly that the Department of Justice must intercede into the questionable practices of the DEA and provide him with the necessary protection to ensure that his life and livelihood are not subjected to ongoing harassment and intimidation.

    Attorney General Reno, Mr Prince has contacted me out of desperation. While in Houston, Texas, I had the opportunity to visit Mr. Prince's buildings and I spoke to his workers.

    After listening to Mr. Prince's concerns, and that of his customers, I suggested that he document his torments at the hands of the DEA agents and send it to you for your perusal. Please understand that Mr. Prince has asked me to assist him because of my work surrounding the intelligence community, police harassment and brutality, and the reported incidents of "driving while black/brown."

    I am often contacted by African Americans who feel helpless when confronted with the incidents as described by Mr. Prince. The harrowing details of Mr. Prince's allegations and my reputation in vigorously pursuing such matters warrants that I assist him to the best of my capabilities. Will you please give this matter your immediate attention? I anxiously await your response.

Sincerely,

Maxine Waters

Maxine Waters
Member of Congress

the illegal search of his automobile, and that his customers are stopped and questioned without provocation by the DEA. Mr. Prince also has raised concerns about the interference in his right to travel, and he has been stopped numerous times on dark stretches of Texas highways. Simply put, Mr. Prince believes strongly that the Department of Justice must intercede into the questionable practices of the DEA and provide him with the necessary protection to ensure that his life and livelihood are not subjected to ongoing harassment and intimidation.

Attorney General Reno, Mr. Prince has contacted me out of desperation. While in Houston, Texas, I had the opportunity to visit Mr. Prince's buildings and I spoke to his workers.

After listening to Mr. Prince's concerns and that of his customers, I suggested that he document his torments at the hands of DEA agents and send it to you for your perusal. Please understand that Mr. Prince has asked me to assist him because of my work surrounding the intelligence community, police harassment and brutality, and the reported incidents of "driving while black/brown."

I am often contacted by African Americans who feel helpless when confronted with the incidents as described by Mr. Prince. The harrowing details of Mr. Prince's allegations and my reputation in vigorously pursuing such matters warrants that I assist him to the best of my capabilities. Will you please give this matter your immediate attention? I anxiously await your response.

Sincerely,
Maxine Waters
Member of Congress

I never met Janet Reno. Nor do I plan to. But it's quite possible that at that point, my fate was in her hands. It was my survival instinct that sent me to Congresswoman Maxine Waters. I'd made it through 34 years on this earth by refusing to be anyone's victim. That had been my attitude when it came to fighting poverty, fighting for my education, and building my businesses, and I was not about to change for law enforcement.

My meeting with Congresswoman Waters officially put my position on record. I wanted everyone – including Attorney General Janet Reno – to know exactly what DEA agents Jack Schumacher and Chad Scott were trying to do. If they tried again, I was fully prepared to defend myself.

Congresswoman Waters' letter to Attorney General Reno set in motion an interesting turn of events at the DEA. The investigation into Rap-A-Lot, and myself, was closed for lack of findings. Agent Jack Schumacher was reassigned to desk duty. Chad Scott was reprimanded when authorities found the Rap-A-Lot jewelry he'd stolen from my promotions team in his desk drawer.

It was more than a decade later when my younger brother Torrey, my mother's son, was murdered in a triple homicide. I received word that Jack Schumacher, now retired, had been down at the sheriff's office snooping around and questioning witnesses. Although he had nothing to do with the case, he was sure that I'd put a bounty out for my brother's killer. He was trying to shift the focus from my brother to me. I guess some habits die hard.

And as for the man in tactical gear in the Cutlass? As I'm writing this, former DEA agent Chad Scott is under federal indictment awaiting trial. He's been accused of stealing cash from drug dealers, lying under oath, and falsifying documents for decades throughout his career. They say God works in mysterious ways. I hope he gets what he deserves, as justice for all the homies' lives that he's ruined.

On the following pages is a portion of my private investigator's report. This report proved invaluable in soliciting the help of Congresswoman Waters and Attorney General Reno when I was being unjustly targeted by the DEA.

August 20, 1999

Mr. ███████
Attorney at Law

███████████████

Re: Rap-A-Lot Records
        James A. Prince
        File No. ███████

REPORT OF INVESTIGATION

Assignment

Our assignment was received on June 21, 1999, and we appreciate our having been so favored. Our assignment was to assist your law firm in gathering evidence to prove that Mr. James A. Prince and Rap-A-Lot Records is, and has been, the long term victim of harassment by local and federal law enforcement.

Mr. James A. Prince

This investigator, in our early conferences, met with Mr. James A. Prince, the CEO of Rap-A-Lot Records. Mr. Prince advised us that since the beginning of his career in music, it is of his opinion, that he has been the target of law enforcement harassment. Mr. Prince believes that law enforcement has come to the conclusion that his financial success, as well as his record label, is that of drug trafficking.

This investigator, after our initial interviews, started reviewing the records at the Harris County Courthouse, and found that as Mr. Prince had stated, that as early as November 1984, Mr. Prince has been stopped, detained, and even arrested on the pretense of a drug related offense. We found there were a total of five documented arrests by law enforcement on all drug related charges, but that none of these had any evidence to prove the alleged charge and all were dismissed. We have below cited each of these charges and have enclosed as attachments, the charge, as well as the dismissal on each of these cases.

Case Number	File Date	Offense	Disposition

Drug Enforcement Agency - DEA

This investigator found that in reviewing Mr. Prince's arrest history in investigations, i appeared that DEA was the agency most actively investigating Mr. Prince. We found however, the IRS, as well as the Houston Police Department, coordinated efforts with DE in efforts to prove up, unsuccessfully, that Mr. Prince was involved in drug trafficking. W found that the lead agent in most of these investigations was a Mr. Jack H. Schumacher, wh is currently employed with the Houston office of DEA. This investigator found that M Schumacher was formerly with the Houston Police Department, where he worked as Detective, before leaving and becoming an agent of the Drug Enforcement Agency. Thi investigator found that Mr. Schumacher, in his law enforcement career, has been responsib for the shooting death of at least eight individuals that he was investigating.

This investigator had an opportunity to talk with people who have worked in the past wit Mr. Schumacher, and they shared on a very confidential basis, that in most cases, M Schumacher has created the situation that resulted in the use of deadly force. In ou discussion, it was made very clear that these people, most who had known Mr. Schumache for almost twenty years, did not want to step forward and place themselves in what the consider imperil with him or any other law enforcement agency.

We were advised that Mr. Schumacher is a very successful investigator, as well as a maste of the sting-type operation. We were told that in Mr. Schumacher's sting operations, h always leaves an open end to the end of his investigation, which always results in somewha of a confrontational type point, that from time to time results in the use of deadly forc where Mr. Schumacher has in the past been able to execute the use of deadly force, resultin in the loss of life of his target subject.

POLITICS & SETUPS

With the help of Maxine Waters, I'd gone on the record saying that I believed my life was in danger, and any continued threats would be met in kind. That meant the determined agents who were willing to bend the law to arrest me could no longer reach out and touch me – at least not directly.

Texas is a large, wealthy state. In 2014, my home state came in third behind New York and California with the number of billionaires on the Forbes 400 list. And where there is money, there's politics. I've never been into politics. Growing up in the hood can be such an isolating experience. You're more concerned with who's running the block than who's running the country. The streets are a union unto themselves. In the Fifth Ward, the world of politics felt inaccessible. The only time politicians ever came to my hood was for a photo op. Let's be honest, every politician knows how awful the living conditions are in the poorest areas. But poverty is profitable for them, so they let it continue.

Congresswoman Maxine Waters intervening on my behalf and contacting Janet Reno was the first time I could ever say a politician helped me, and that wasn't until I was 34 years old. So the political process was never as important to me as on-the-ground action. I'd become a millionaire both in the streets and in the corporate world without ever once exercising my right to vote. I'm not knocking the process, nor am I encouraging others not to vote. I'm simply saying that in my life, having seen this country use my tax dollars to go to war against me, voting is not something I'm led to do. Neither is supporting the politicians. The latest election of Donald Trump in 2016, who received three million less votes than his opponent, underscores the reality of the American electoral system. Your vote doesn't always count.

Shortly after the DEA reassigned Jack Schumacher to desk duty, *The Dallas Morning News* published the first of a series of articles about me. First, they reported that the DEA's investigation had been dropped because of political pressure from Washington. In my opinion, it was dropped because it had gone on for years and they still hadn't found anything. The newspaper didn't report that it was continual harassment and an invasion of my privacy. The newspaper painted Jack Schumacher as a decorated agent doing his job, not someone who was a danger to my personal safety. *The Dallas Morning News* ran articles dissecting Scarface's lyrics, implying that some of his aggressive songs were legitimate threats against police officers and federal agents. At first, I couldn't understand why the city of Dallas was suddenly so interested in me.

It wasn't unusual for my pastor, Ralph West, to inform me when the church was expecting a notable visitor. So in 1999, when he told me that Vice President Al Gore would be visiting The Church Without Walls, I didn't think anything was out of the ordinary. I knew the political power of the Black church, specifically *our* church, and at the time, Gore was in the middle of his Presidential campaign. I was invited to a meet-and-greet session after the church services, but I felt no differently about him than any other politician.

On the morning of his visit, my family and I arrived at church at the same time as usual. But as we pulled into our normal parking spot, I noticed the Secret Service. Of course, anytime someone from the White House moves around, the Secret Service is to be expected. But these guys looked different. Something felt odd. Their attention was on me as I drove up. As we walked inside and sat in the same place we sat every Sunday, I felt their eyes on me. Secret Service agents were everywhere, and judging from their body language, I felt certain they were watching me.

Meeting the Vice President wasn't important enough for me to ignore the feeling that I was being set up. I felt bad energy all around me from these agents, and I didn't hang around to meet Al Gore. We left just prior to the benediction.

Less than a week later, *The Dallas Morning News* ran a story alleging that I donated $200,000 to Gore's election campaign. I never even voted. Why would I give money to a man I didn't even wait 15 minutes to meet? By now it should be clear to everyone the value I place on a dollar. Throughout my life, money has represented freedom and power. I've fought and sacrificed more than I'd ever care to talk about, and I've always stayed dedicated to the streets, to the forgotten neighborhoods that kept me in business when law enforcement agencies were trying to shut me down. So believe me when I tell you I'd ride through the hood tossing $200,000 in twenty dollar bills out the window before I'd give it to a politician I didn't know anything about. But that didn't stop *The Dallas Morning News* from running the story, and other news outlets picked it up.

I didn't know what to make of it until I realized the connection. In the previous presidential election, Bill Clinton - with Al Gore as his running mate - had defeated Ross Perot. It definitely was NOT coincidental that Ross Perot was from Dallas, and *The Dallas Morning News* was suddenly interested in reporting on me constantly. Ross Perot was attempting to gain some political advantage by using my situation to smear Al Gore and Maxine Waters' names.

One day, I got a call from my publicist telling me to turn on C-SPAN. As I sat there in my office in Houston, the House Committee on Government Reform was holding a hearing in Washington, D.C. to determine if Rap-A-Lot Records was a criminal organization, with me as its mastermind.

In the streets, when someone has beef with you, they bring it to your front door. Even if they don't come to you directly, they make enough noise that you have no choice but to come to them. I was used to dealing with those kinds of adversaries. There's a strange sense of honor in direct confrontation. But how can you deal with an opponent who basically holds a trial against you and you're not even invited to attend?

For two days I sat in my office and watched the hearing. At times it felt surreal, like they were talking about someone else. Other times I felt vindicated. Through the DEA transcripts and recorded conversations that were introduced at the hearing, I learned that there were specific times when they had been clocking my movements. One of those instances was the Sunday that Al Gore visited my church. My instincts had been right.

I've been investigated for criminal wrongdoing and charged twelve times throughout my adult life, and I've beaten every accusation. But there's an inevitable feeling of resentment and distrust that comes each time you see "The United States of America vs. James Prince" written on a sheet of paper.

When the hearing concluded, several media outlets reached out to me for a comment. I figured if the very government fighting against me wasn't interested in what I had to say, why should I give my thoughts to the press?

I've always lived my life in the middle of God's hand, surrounded by a sea of ants. Throughout my life, those thousands of ants have always wanted nothing more than to eat me alive. Trust me when I tell you, some have gotten mighty close. But just when it looks like there might be serious trouble for me, God closes His fingers, keeping me safe. And these hearings were no different. So I didn't have a comment to give. Why should I? Those hearings weren't for me; they were for *them*. The United States government has spent millions of dollars trying to stop me from succeeding, and they still haven't gotten it right. Because if God is for you, who can be against you?

BOXING: MY FIRST LOVE

Ever since childhood, I've been in love with the sport of boxing. I never forgot the fighting techniques the older guys taught me while I was growing up in Fifth Ward. There weren't any gyms in my neighborhood, so slap-boxing with the neighborhood guys was the next best thing. At the time it felt like play, until I came to need those skills in the real world. Then I realized it had been a blessing. But more than anything, it was interacting with men. If time is the first thing you're robbed of in the hood, then quality time with adults is second. The first priority of impoverished people is survival, and everything else falls in line after that. As a child, having a chance to learn from the older guys and interact with them through boxing made me feel important and acknowledged.

Once I became a successful adult, that acknowledgement was what I wanted to give back to the youth of the Fifth Ward. I had become a millionaire, brought my family out of poverty, and built Rap-A-Lot into a thriving record label which was changing the way people thought about the South. But I wanted to do more. I always remembered that night when I was nine years old and my Aunt Teddy called me a "peculiar" child, chosen by God.

It was late one night, shortly after 4 AM, when I shot straight up in my bed. God had placed an idea on my heart to build a boxing gym in the Fifth Ward. It would be a place where any child could come and learn to box and get some physical activity, but most importantly, where they would feel acknowledged.

I found some land on Jensen Drive that was up for sale and we broke ground. For the most part, the city supported me, but I did encounter some push back. After cutting through a lot of red tape, we got the building up. The Prince Complex opened its doors in the Fifth Ward, less than two miles from where I used to slap-box on the corner. But I knew this was just the beginning.

The more time I spent in the boxing gym, the more my love for the sport came back to me. Boxing was always my first love; music just got in the way. Finally, I decided to pursue it. Now, don't get me wrong, I wasn't under any delusion that I could become a professional fighter, but I knew enough about the sport and the business to become a successful boxing manager. So I asked God to send me a champion fighter.

At the time, Mike Tyson was the biggest fighter, the undisputed heavyweight champion of the world. At 20 years old he became the youngest fighter to win the WBC, WBA and IBF heavyweight titles. No one would dispute that he was a champion. And I wanted in. Why not go for the best?

Coming from where I'm from, and having dealt with guys in the streets as well as rap artists, I wasn't concerned about Mike Tyson's legal issues. No matter what, Mike was an amazing fighter, and I knew there were opportunities that his current manager wasn't exploring. Through some mutual acquaintances, I set up a meeting in Las Vegas to discuss the possibility of joining his management team. It's not uncommon for an athlete or artist to have a team of people managing their careers.

As soon as I got to Vegas, I went straight to Mike's gym to watch the work out. While watching Mike fight, my friend and I were approached by another boxer who acknowledged me for my accomplishments in music. He was a smaller guy, closer to my size than Mike's, and he wanted to talk to me about music. I took his number but I wasn't that interested because I had come there to meet with Mike.

After the workout, we all sat down and I explained to Mike what I could bring to the table. Strategy and negotiation have always been my strengths. Mike liked what he heard. He put his wife on the phone and told her he wanted me to be a part of his team. By the end of the meeting, we'd reached an agreement and shook hands.

The next morning, Mike Tyson's phone number had been changed. He wasn't at the gym and I had no way of getting in touch with him. See, boxing is a business like every other business. And just as I learned in music, the old guys don't always welcome new blood. Shelly Finkel is a longtime boxing manager who, like me, started in music. At the time, he was managing Mike and viewed me as a threat. I believe that he didn't want to cut me in on the deal. When he found out Mike had taken the meeting, I think he put the brakes on the entire situation.

I had gone to Vegas to sign my champion fighter, and now it looked like I was leaving with nothing. As we packed up, I turned to my friend and asked about the other fighter who approached us in the gym. My friend handed me the piece of paper with his contact information and told me he was a 130-pound champion. I decided to give him a call before I hopped on a flight back to Houston. His name was Floyd Mayweather.

MONEY & MAYWEATHER

When Floyd Mayweather has his mind made up, he moves quickly. It didn't take long for us to reach a deal. Initially, Floyd wanted to talk about music. He'd been making his own songs and wanted to get into the record industry, but I knew from our first official meeting that my focus with Floyd should be in the ring.

This was 2000, and Floyd was 23 years old. His managers at the time were his father Floyd Sr. and his uncle, Jeff Mayweather. They were all from a long line of boxers and knew the sport like no one else. But when it came to business, Floyd Jr. wasn't being given the tools he needed to take him to the next level. That's where I came in.

Immediately, my involvement created tension between Floyd and his father and uncle. After looking over his whole infrastructure, I realized that Floyd wasn't in control of any of his money. That's a huge red flag, when the person who makes the money doesn't control the money. So my first order of business was to change that.

Floyd's promoter, Bob Arum, is a longtime boxing promoter. He's organized fights for everyone: Muhammad Ali, Oscar De La Hoya, Manny Pacquiao, Tommy Herns, Julio Caesar Chavez, Sugar Ray Leonard, George Foreman. Bob is a shrewd businessman, and the last thing he wanted was for me to come in shaking things up. He didn't take me seriously in the beginning. In fact, he talked a lot about me in the press; he said he was worried that I didn't have what it took to manage a champion. But the last thing I was worried about was Bob Arum.

Shortly after I came on board, my name started appearing in all of the boxing columns. Floyd Jr. and Sr. were arguing with each other in the press, and sports writers somehow got the idea that I was the cause. I'll be the first to admit I chose business opportunities which are more likely to make money, but I never get involved unless I believe I can make the situation better. I told Floyd Sr. the same thing one night when we all went out to dinner. The public war between Floyd Jr. and Sr. didn't sit right with me. Where I'm from, you honor your mother and your father, you don't diss them in the press. So I told Bob Arum we needed to schedule a meeting with Floyd Sr. and Jr. to get them to agree not to bash each other publicly. Bob and I, along with Bob's stepson Todd DuBoef, arranged the meeting to call a truce.

At the meeting, it seemed like everyone at the table thought I had brainwashed Floyd Jr. First, Floyd Sr. began reading from a list he could hardly see. Bob Arum passed him his glasses. Then, Floyd Sr. asked me, "What did you give my son to sign him? He had a $12 million dollar deal on the table. Your lifestyle is set. He hasn't made his money yet!"

I told him, "I'm not here to discuss the agreement I have with Floyd. But if it's okay with Floyd, I will." Floyd Jr. stepped in and said, "No, we're not here for that." Floyd Sr., who is also a former fighter, grew more upset and started walking in my direction. I told him, "Mr. Mayweather, sir, you seem to be getting upset. But I want you to know I can't take no punches," meaning, it wasn't a good idea for him to come too close to me without there being some consequences. Floyd Jr. immediately understood what I was saying, jumped up, approached his dad, and began taking his jacket off. Suddenly, I found myself standing between the two Floyds. Floyd Jr. and I left to prevent a tragedy. After all the drama, there was no truce.

But I was making Floyd's situation better, even if his father, uncle or promoter didn't think so. Floyd's mother came to me within the first six months of joining the team and told me, "I really appreciate you coming into my son's life. He's never been able to stand up to his father, he's always been too fearful. And now I see him standing up for himself."

Floyd saw improvements right away. He had been frustrated with a number of deals that had been in place before I got there. Floyd Jr.'s biggest frustration was with HBO. The cable network had offered a $12.5 million contract for seven fights. He rejected the offer, telling the press it was a "slave contract," but Floyd Sr. and Bob Arum thought it was a good deal. Bob put Floyd Jr. on the phone with Lou DiBella from HBO to try to make the deal work, but the call didn't go too well. Lou later told the press that it would be a long time before he talked to

Floyd Mayweather again.

Floyd Sr. came to me to fix the HBO deal. All he kept saying was, "He needs to take the deal." Floyd Sr. thought that because I was already wealthy, I wasn't in a rush to make the HBO deal happen. But what it really meant was that I know how to make money. The first rule of making money is that you don't take just any old thing that's offered to you. Of course, $12.5 million is in no way a "slave contract." There are people who have to work an entire week for twelve dollars. So the fact that Floyd had said that didn't sit well with me. But although I didn't agree with the way he handled it, my job was to figure out a creative way to increase the $12.5 million they were offering him. We needed HBO as an ally, but HBO was ticked off. To punish Floyd, they gave him a fight against Emanuel Burton on a brand-new HBO boxing showcase called KO Nation. It was a tough fight, but we got through it. The purse was for $250,000. It was the price Floyd had to pay for his comments. I had my work cut out for me.

Floyd's fight with Gregorio Vargas was his first fight with me as his manager. Under the existing deal, which Bob Arum had put in place, Floyd was only going to make $750,000. Now, I know to most of you reading this, $750,000 for one night seems like a lot of money. But let me break it down to you like this: you're not being paid for one night's work. It takes months to train for a fight. Sometimes it might even take a year. We're talking about 365 days of strict dieting and brutal physical conditioning, and none of this is a solo effort. You still have to pay your trainer, other specialists, other fighters and their assistants, nutritionists, and a private chef. And don't forget the gym; you need a facility which is ready and available every second of the day. All that takes money.

Then, there's also the risk factor. Every time a fighter steps into the ring, there's a high probability that he won't come out the same. Although boxing is a sport that relies on skill and technique, it's also one of the riskiest. Fighters risk their lives every single bout, and they have to be compensated for that risk. So when you add up all those factors, you've reached a number. That number is the value of the fighter. Now, jump to the other side and look at how much the promoter is making by selling out the arena. Then add all of the money the network is making by televising the fight, either directly on their channel or in a deal with Pay-Per-View. Then add up the additional money being earned by selling advertising space in the arena and even within the ring. Now weigh how much money HBO stands to make off of Floyd Mayweather against how much money they felt he was worth as a fighter. $750,000 – even in 2000 – was good. But we wanted better.

Floyd was a million plus fighter. He knew it and I knew it, and it was my job to make sure everyone else knew it. The first thing I did was go around Bob Arum. Lou DiBella was still fuming over the shouting match with Floyd, so I had to go directly to the head of HBO, Seth Abraham. He didn't want to be dealing with me any more than Lou DiBella did. Abraham called me "the most talked about guy in boxing." I asked him why he said that, and he replied, "I got everyone calling about you, from Don King to Bob Arum." Abraham knew talent, both inside the ring and out, and he knew I'd be a force to reckon with. But Abraham wasn't sure if Floyd was worth any additional money. After we talked a bit, I got him to agree to some benchmarks, meaning that if Floyd hit certain markers, he'd be paid an additional $250,000. He agreed, and Floyd hit them. His victory over Vargas became his first million-dollar fight.

Shortly after that, Floyd fired his father as both his manager and his trainer. Now that I had Floyd's trust, HBO's attention, and the necessary control, I set out to get Floyd a better contract. In order for a boxer to make a huge payday they have to be a Pay-Per-View star, meaning their name has to draw the people to their screens to order the fight. HBO had a special interest in Diego Corrales, a super featherweight IBF champion who was probably one of the most dangerous fighters in Floyd's division. Diego was ranked #1 and had an impressive 33-0 record with 27 TKOs. Floyd was ranked #2. HBO said that if Floyd could beat Corrales, that $12.5 million offer would double, if not triple.

Floyd wanted no parts of Diego, but I had a plan to not only prepare Floyd but also to get inside Diego's head. Always know who you're fighting, no matter the arena. A little bit of homework can give you the advantage and make the difference between a big win and a big loss. Diego was a champion inside the ring, but outside, he was in some trouble. He'd been arrested for a domestic battery incident; he allegedly fractured the skull of his pregnant wife during an argument. I tried telling Floyd to take the opportunity to beat Diego for every battered woman in America. That still wasn't enough for Floyd, and I talked to him for several hours, trying to get him to be in agreement with me. Finally, around six in the morning, I gave up and went home and went to sleep. A few hours later I woke up to a voicemail from Floyd, saying, "I hired you to guide my career, so if you think this is the right time for the fight, then let's fight." Now that I had Floyd in agreement, I called

HBO, but they wouldn't give us a fight date. Lou DiBella was still stung from the bad press surrounding the contract offer, so they claimed all of their fight dates were full. I knew I would have to get creative.

It was November of 2000 and Lennox Lewis had a fight against David Tua that weekend; it was the perfect opportunity to make some noise. There's an art to applying public pressure. We showed up, surrounding Diego Corrales at the press conference. Floyd got in his face, telling him he was going to beat him like Diego had beat his wife. We were careful to keep them apart just enough to make sure a free fight didn't break out. But that did the trick. The near-scuffle was all anybody could talk about, and HBO set a date. Floyd had two months to prepare and I had two months to break down Diego.

I kicked off the first press conference by telling Diego Corrales that I had saved two front row seats for his ex-wife Maria and her new boyfriend. I told him Floyd was going to whoop him for every battered woman in the United States of America. I told him he would be going to jail after the fight for what he'd done to his wife. I came out swinging because I needed to get into his head. Boxing is not only a game of technique and skill but also mental toughness. You have to be in control of your thoughts in order to stay focused. Boxers try to block out most of their personal issues in the weeks leading up to the fight. Any distractions could mean disaster in the ring. So my strategy was to keep Diego as distracted as possible. I taunted him relentlessly, and he fell for it. While I handled Diego, Floyd trained. He'd never trained harder. For the first time in his career he knew he had a team he could trust, and all he had to worry about was his performance.

The fight itself was brutal. Even distracted, Diego was a bulldog. Floyd dropped him five times, winning every round, but Diego kept coming. Finally, after the fifth knockdown, Diego's corner man climbed in the ropes and stopped the fight. He had to make that decision for him because Diego was prepared to die in the ring. That night in January 2001, Floyd Mayweather came one giant step closer to becoming a bona fide Pay-Per-View star. It was the beginning of Money Mayweather. It was also the beginning of my interest in Diego Corrales.

DIEGO CORRALES

THE ART & SCIENCE OF
respect

My fight with Big Carl in the second grade was a no-brainer. Sure, he was much bigger than I was, and his record was undefeated, just like mine. But despite logic, it never occurred to me *not* to fight. Fighting is just what I do. It's how I was built. It's in my heart. And there's a lot of people like that. Not just physical fighters, but people who are simply programmed to keep going. In spite of the odds being stacked against me with local, state, and federal agencies trying to lock me up, I couldn't stop fighting. Larry Hoover had been locked up for 27 years and he still wasn't broken, and he told me, "No matter what, don't stop swinging." He wasn't just saying it, he was - and still is - living it. So in spite of being born handicapped into poverty, fear, and illiteracy, I was able to push through and rise above the limitations of my surroundings. There's something in a select few of us that keeps us going. There's no off switch. And as long as there's breath in our lungs, we'll keep pushing. So even though Diego Corrales was our opponent during his fight with Floyd Mayweather, I knew he was one of *us*.

Watching Diego fight was like watching a pitbull keep charging. Even as they declared Floyd the winner, catapulting him to the next level, I couldn't help but think about Diego. Any fighter with that much heart is someone I wanted to manage.

A few months after the fight with Floyd, Diego was sentenced to two years in prison for assault on his ex-wife Maria. We all make bad choices, and Diego was paying for his. But I wanted to be there to help him move forward when he got out. I reached out to Diego's fiancé Michelle and told her flat-out that I wanted to be in business with him. She told me Diego hated me and it would never happen; she said Diego would try to fight me if he ever saw me again. Nevertheless, I convinced her to take me to the prison to meet Diego face to face, to explain my actions.

Michelle had to trick Diego into meeting with me. She came during her normal visiting time but never mentioned that she'd be bringing his sworn enemy. She knew she was doing the right thing, because Diego needed some guidance. He wouldn't be in prison forever, and she felt that working with me would be the best option for her husband and her family. Diego didn't see it that way. At first, he didn't have much to say. But then another well-respected inmate with street cred came over and asked if he could shake my hand. He turned to Diego and told him he was lucky to have me as a visitor. Diego warmed up a lot after that, and this allowed me time to explain myself. "Listen, I did what I had to do to help Floyd win," I told him. I explained that the mind games were never anything personal against Diego, it was just business. Since Floyd was my fighter, I had a responsibility to him to do whatever's necessary to help him win. I explained that I'd have that same responsibility to Diego if he'd trust me enough to let me manage him. Like I told Floyd, I told Diego I didn't want to get involved in any situation unless I believe I could make it better. Diego signed his management contract right there in prison.

Diego was released from prison about a year later and we went to work immediately. I knew I had to start over with him. He'd been a million-dollar fighter before he went to jail, but was released from his Top Rank contract when he was released from prison. You can't blame Top Rank, he'd been gone for a long time. They didn't know what kind of fighter they were getting. So the first few fights after his release brought him only $20,000 to $30,000, but we stuck it out. Diego brought that same heart to his training. He worked harder than anyone else and trusted me to guide his career.

In May of 2005, Diego defeated Jose Luis Castillo by TKO to win his fourth title belt. It was a phenomenal fight, and many regarded it as the fight of the decade. This was a victory for us both. He was a million-dollar fighter once again, and he'd given it his all. Exactly two years later on the same date and almost at the same exact time he beat Castillo, Diego was killed while riding his motorcycle in Las Vegas.

I don't think I've had a more fulfilling journey than working with Diego Corrales. I was honored that I got to work with him.

PRINCE VS. KING

THE ART & SCIENCE OF
respect

"Prince, brotha, I'm glad that a REAL nigga is in this business. Me and you, brotha, we need to get together." This was the first time I ever spoken to Don King, but after my success with Floyd, my name was buzzing throughout the boxing world, so I wasn't surprised by his phone call. "I know when these white folks ain't saying nothing good about you, you must be handling your business," he told me. "We need to get together."

Our chance to get together came a few months later when I was asked to manage a world champion fighter by the name of James Page. Page started fighting as a young kid in California. He was a good guy, but always had a dark side to him, and had been in trouble with the law. Six months after turning pro, Page, who was only 19, was arrested for stealing from the gym where he trained. He served 10 months in San Quentin.

When Page got out of prison in 1998, he vowed to focus on his boxing career and turn his life around. He signed a promotional deal with Don King and a management deal with Don's son Carl. Now, you don't have to be a legal, business or boxing expert to know that being managed by the son of your promoter is a conflict of interest. Page still won and defended the welterweight championship three times, but eventually money became an issue.

Page came to me on recommendation from a friend. He was being underpaid for his fights and dropped Carl as his manager. I wasn't worried about his legal trouble, but I was concerned about his drinking. But I agreed to work with him anyway. I liked James as a fighter and I saw the potential in him, plus, I was excited to work with Don King, who still held Page's contract as a promoter.

By this time, Page was trying to make a comeback. He'd been stripped of his world title by not showing up for a mandatory fight in 2001 and needed to beat Andrew "Six Heads" Lewis in order to regain it. Showtime picked up the fight as a part of an Evander Holyfield undercard for $500,000 and proposed to pay Page $70,000. So I reached out to Don in an effort to increase the amount. "Let us eat a little more," was what I said to Don over the phone. I'd watched his moves for years, and even though he was controversial, he was a shrewd businessman and I'd learned a thing or two from him. So I reached out to Don, one "real nigga" to another, the same man who had expressed his excitement for me entering the boxing world earlier. Only now that I was asking for money, I was a little *too* real.

"If you want more to eat, you better get it from somewhere else," Don King told me. He wasn't willing to play ball, so I had to get creative. It just so happened that a few days before the fight, James Page hurt his hands while sparring and the bout had to be cancelled. This was a loss for us, even moreso for Don King, who also promoted Six Heads. If the fight had taken place, Six Heads' contract with Don King would've automatically extended. But the cancellation meant that Six Heads was now a free agent, and the fight with James Page went up for purse bid.

Bob Arum's Top Rank won the bid to promote the fight between James Page and Six Heads, which now left Don King all the way out of the picture – a position Don's not used to being in. When two promoters don't agree over the amount of a fight, the fight gets auctioned off to the highest promoter. So Bob agreed to pay James Page a higher fee and signed Six Heads to a new promotions contract, and things seemed to be back on track.

I brought James Page to Houston to train for the fight, but we soon discovered that he was slipping off at night to smoke crack. I wanted to help him, and I wanted my fighter in the best shape possible, but despite my attempts, the damage to his body and mind had already been done. He lost the fight to Six Heads, not only losing his chance to regain his title, but also blowing an opportunity to move on to the million-dollar fight I'd set up against "Sugar" Shane Mosley. Page was devastated; he'd lost everything. And Don King was right there to strike while Page was down. He convinced the fighter to join him in a $20 million lawsuit against me for tortious interference, claiming I interfered with his track record of successful fights with Showtime. During the trial in New York, it was revealed that Don had been double dipping with James Page the entire time his son Carl served as Page's manager. I won the case and the headlines read, "The Prince Defeats

The King." Business went up after that.

James Page received the biggest payday of his career while working with me, but Don King never worked with him again after losing that lawsuit. And Page – for some reason, which no one understands – started robbing banks wearing nothing but some reading glasses and a button-down shirt. He even drove his own car. The FBI dubbed him the "Button Down Bandit"; he was sentenced to seven years in prison. I felt bad for him and sent him some money in jail. Addiction is a sad and dangerous thing.

(Below) A 2001 news article about my court battle with Don King

The Prince Defeats The King
by Fiona Manning (November 20, 2001)

In a landmark jury verdict, rap mogul and boxing manager James Prince has defeated a $20-million law suit launched against him by promoter Don King, who sued industry newcomer for "interference in his relationship with former WBA welterweight champion James Page". King lost the case on a unanimous jury verdict last month.

In fact, the jury felt King had provided no evidence of tort and that his attack on Prince was so malicious, they told defendant Prince they would have awarded him $1 million damages if they had been allowed to do so.

Prince should be happy, but now King has filed an appeal against the verdict, despite the fact that both the judge presiding over the case and the jury said there was "not a scintilla of evidence supporting King's claim."

"It's an inconvenience more than anything," said Prince told MaxBoxing.com. "I fully believe more than anything that King's true intention here was to find out exactly how much money I have and I am happy to say he did not."

MIKE TYSON vs. ROY JONES JR.

I'm a businessman, and a businessman is most loyal to the money. So even while Rap-A-Lot was booming, I was always looking for my next venture. One of the best ways to identify potential opportunities is to stay in tune with what your peers are doing. The people you surround yourself with determine exactly how far you're going to go. Staying in the company of people who aren't doing much limits your network. So I try to always make sure I'm surrounded by people as dedicated and driven as I am.

Roy Jones is one of those people. We met years ago, after he said that Scarface was his favorite rapper. He's someone I considered a friend, because we have many things in common. We're both from the South, and share a love for hunting, fishing, music and, of course, boxing. Roy understands the importance of good business, and we can discuss different ideas. And we almost made history together.

It was around 2002 when I had the idea to put together a super fight between Roy Jones Jr. and Mike Tyson. Roy had just made history by becoming the first Middleweight title holder to ever become the Heavyweight Champion of the World, and he was still undefeated. This was before Mike Tyson was knocked out by Lennox Lewis, so his buzz was still high. He was hungry and looking for another shot at the title. Even though my attempt to manage him had been a failure, I liked Mike and still wanted to help him win any way I could. The timing was perfect.

Roy and Mike came out to my ranch in Texas to meet with me about the idea of the fight. I showed them around the property and all three of us caught up with one another. It was a great day. Finally, we retreated to my office to get down to business. When it came down to the terms, the concern was money. Bottom line. Both men were at a premium, and we knew this fight would be the one to watch. $25 million apiece was the goal they both agreed on. We all shook on it and they left. Then we went to work to find the $50 million.

We needed publicity; a fight of this magnitude had to be announced in a big way. It was the Hip Hop era, and both Roy and Mike love Hip Hop and collaborated with rappers as much as possible. So we reached out to my friend Dave Mays, who owned *The Source Magazine* at the time. *The Source* had been considered Hip Hop's bible, and right away, Dave understood the value this fight would have to his audience. The Source Awards were coming up and Dave agreed to let Roy and Mike present an award together, as an opportunity to announce the fight. This would kick off the buzz in a major way. And with a televised announcement already in place, we were in a better position to find the money.

Joe and Gavin Maloof are Las Vegas-based businessmen whose family made their fortune distributing Coors beer in the 1930s. Since then they've invested in many things, including the Palms Casino Resort, films and television shows, NBA franchises, and professional boxing matches. We reached out to them to underwrite the fight, hoping they'd guarantee the $25 million apiece that Roy and Mike agreed upon plus the upside of the Pay-Per-View sales. Our meeting in Las Vegas went well and the Maloofs understood the value of the fight, but were only willing to guarantee $17 million apiece to each fighter. And they weren't budging.

Mike was all in. $17 million was still a good deal, and the upside from the Pay-Per-View would make this an easy profit no matter who won or lost. But Roy wasn't having it. He'd agreed to $25 million and felt that anything less than that was below his value. Nothing could change his mind.

Finally, Roy accepted a rematch with Antonio Tarver instead in May 2004. I remember watching that fight; I remember the exact moment when Tarver's knockout punch landed in the second round. As Roy fell, so did our monster fight between two undisputed heavyweights. The three of us were supposed to make history together. It took one minute and 42 seconds to lose the opportunity - and to lose $17 million dollars. There aren't many moments in my career that I've lost sleep over, but that night, it was impossible to find rest.

MONEY ON THE TABLE

A rtists and athletes are very similar. The passion they have for their music or their sport is evident in the time and effort they put towards making it better. Whether it's body conditioning and learning plays, or vocal rehearsals and writing songs, all that time and effort is what earns their success. But the thing that many artists and athletes never master is business.

I've made a lot of money with some of the most talented individuals on the planet. But I've also watched some of those same individuals miss out on opportunities because they either didn't learn the ins and outs of the business or didn't trust me to guide them through it.

The first thing I did when I entered the world of professional boxing was align myself with proven champions, both in and out of the ring, so I could learn from the best. Roy Jones Jr. has become a great ally in this business. His expertise as a fighter is followed closely by his expertise as a promoter and a businessman. And although I've butted heads with Bob Arum over the years, we still built a bond and have done some great deals together. But when you're dealing with a fighter, a manager, and a promoter, it's very easy for things to get off course. And it's usually the fighter who suffers.

Winky Wright was a fighter I came to manage after watching him lose to Antonio Vargas. In my opinion, Winky won, but he didn't get the judge's decision. He was also grossly undervalued. At the time, the most he'd made for a fight was $100,000, but I knew he was worth much more. I signed him to a management deal and then immediately signed him to a joint venture with Bob Arum's Top Rank and Roy Jones' Square Ring. By doing a joint venture with both promotions companies, Winky had access to Roy Jones' undercards and Bob Arum's reach.

Overnight, Winky became a million-dollar fighter. Winky fought three bouts on Roy's undercard, each time taking a small fee while delivering a win. So when we were offered a fight with "Sugar" Shane Mosley, for $500,000, I turned it down. He'd earned a reputation as a fighter that could deliver, and needed to be paid as such. In business, you set your own value by delivering. How much you're paid is determined by the choices you made. And when you aren't being compensated for the work you put in, you make different choices. That didn't sit too well with Bob, so I convinced Roy to buy him out of Winky's contract. I knew we could get the same fight somewhere else, but with more money. And that's exactly what we did. After Winky beat Sugar Shane, the door was open for Winky Wright vs. Felix Trinidad. This was the last fight on my contract with Winky and when he won, it was fulfilling for me to see how much he'd grown not only as a fighter but also as a brand. But Winky didn't share my sentiment. He opted not to renew his contract with me and abandoned his contract with Roy, opting instead to be represented by his longtime family attorney. A few fights later he was set up to fight Bernard Hopkins, where he got demolished. His career never recovered. I would've never let that happen.

I got the idea to put together a fight for Sugar Shane and Manny Pacquiao. This was in 2011, after Shane had already beaten Oscar De La Hoya, twice. This was a good time for him, but the reactions to the idea were mixed. Bob told me it'd never happen. Shane was signed to Golden Boy Promotions, the company founded by Oscar De La Hoya. But I pressed Bob for the bottom line: if I could deliver Shane, would he give us a fight? Bob said yes.

Turns out "Sugar" Shane Mosley wasn't just signed as a fighter with Golden Boy Promotions, he was a partner too. Partnership in a company means you have an ownership stake. Most people are offered a percentage in exchange for the ability for the company to leverage whatever you have to offer. Sugar Shane's leverage was his fights. But he wasn't seeing much of a return. In several years as a partner, Sugar Shane had only made $17,000 with the promotional company, which was hailed as one of the most profitable in the business. He wasn't even seeing much benefit as a fighter. Golden Boy offered him a little over $100,000 to fight Canello Alvarez, a fight which was worth far more than the pennies they put on the table. Sugar Shane allowed my team to look over his contract.

I tried to explain to Sugar Shane the disservice he was doing to himself by sacrificing and taking such a tremendous risk for someone else's brand with such little reward. Just as Oscar had a responsibility to his people and his family, Sugar Shane had the same responsibility to his own. Shane was onboard. This was where the business came in. Per Shane's signed contract, the only way he could fight outside of Golden Boy was by relinquishing his partnership in the company, even though his promotional agreement as a fighter had expired. The fault here wasn't with Golden Boy. As a business, their job is to protect their business. Shane's lawyer had advised him to sign a one-sided deal that not only affected his career as a fighter but also wasn't very profitable for him as a partner. But ultimately, that was Shane's fault.

Jay-Z has a line that says, "I'm not a businessman. I'm a business, man." When you're an entity, your first job is to make sure your art or your skill is at the professional level. Your second job is to make sure you've surrounded yourself with qualified people who are on the same page and will do what's best on your behalf. Your third job is to stay on top of them.

We got Sugar Shane out of his partnership deal, and now he was a free agent. I went back to Bob Arum. Bob kept his word and gave us the Pacquiao fight, which guaranteed $5 million with a substantial upside from the Pay-Per-View. But no matter how good your business is, nothing can account for fate. Shortly before the fight, Sugar Shane tore his Achilles tendon while playing in a charity basketball game. He wasn't 100% healed by the time the fight came around and lost to Manny Pacquiao. Still, a year later, Sugar Shane fought Canello Alvarez - a fight I got him – for over $1 million dollars. Then we set up a million-dollar Anthony Mundine fight, which got complicated. The deal with Mundine's promoter was for $300,000.00 upfront, with the remaining $700,000.00 due ten days before the fight. But less than 24 hours before the bout, we still hadn't been paid. I told Shane to hop on the next flight home and pocket the $300,000. The following year Mundine circled back with a new promoter and made the same $1 million dollar deal. This time, the fight went forward. Shane lost, but he retired a multimillionaire.

As I said, if I can't make the situation better, I don't want to be involved. All I expect is, if I have made your situation better, you compensate me. That was where Floyd and I ran afoul.

Floyd came out of the Diego Corrales fight a bona fide star. There's a lot that comes with that. Your endorsement deals change; your access to just about everything increases, and if you're not careful, your ego balloons. And everyone knows that Floyd has an ego. But everyone loved him, even HBO. Together we were able to flip their original $12 million offer into a contract that's worth anywhere from $24 to $50 million, factoring in the incentives. At the very least, we'd doubled their original offer. Floyd had no complaints, and that's why I'm not sure why he had such an issue paying me. Floyd didn't want his last fight to happen under contract with me because he flat out didn't want to compensate me for all of the hard work I put in. He mistook my kindness for weakness and was fooling himself. Things between us became distant. Communication was at an all-time low, and he was trying to avoid paying my $600,000 fee, so I flew to Las Vegas to settle it in person.

When I arrived at the training facilities where Floyd was working out, the mood was tense. After his training, he and I stepped aside and I attempted to talk with him man to man. I wanted to know why he wasn't paying me. Floyd mentioned settling things in court, and I told him I was there to hold court. In the midst of us talking, a brawl had broken out between his guys and my guys. After he realized that paying me was the right thing to do, he gave me his word that he would pay me and we all walked away. To his credit, Floyd kept his word, and he had Bob Arum pay his debt. It was done.

Fightnews.com NEWS | RANKINGS | INTERVIEWS

Floyd Mayweather speaks!

By Karl Freitag

The WBC Jr lightweight champion spoke to Fightnews.com about the bad blood between him and his Saturday opponent Diego Corrales, his controversial "slave contract" statement and his manager James Prince.

On the feud with Diego Corrales:
"This is how everything started. He spoke on the problems with my father, which he shouldn't have spoke on. So I bounced back. I spoke on something that was going on with him. But he couldn't take it

"He totally disrespected me when he walks around talking about how he's going to kill me...I don't wish death to no man. I'm going to expose him. I'm going to show the world that he's not what everybody thinks he is."

On the "HBO slave contract" comment:
"What I said was that the contract they tried to give me "compared to Prince Naseem's contract" was a slave contract. But not saying it in a racist way. That's exactly what I said. They took it and blew it out of proportion."

On manager James Prince:
"Before I went with James Prince, I was making six figures, now I'm making seven figures. Before I hooked up with Jay Prince, I was staying in a $250,000 home. Now I'm staying in a million dollar home. Before James Prince I had a Lexus. Now I've got a Benz and a Corvette. ...James Prince has helped me manage my money and make the right moves."

ANDRE WARD: FAITH & BUSINESS

Andre Ward was a young fighter out of Oakland who had a strong buzz. He's from a boxing family; his father started him in the sport when he was nine years old. But by the time I came across him, in 2000, he was 17 and it appeared his passion for the sport was declining. His godfather was a trainer out of the Bay Area named Virgil Hunter. Virgil was confident Andre could fulfill his tremendous potential, but was having a hard time keeping him focused. Virgil promised that if I could step in and help save Andre from the streets, he'd win a gold medal.

It was rumored that Andre had been blowing off matches. It doesn't matter how good of a fighter you are, once you're considered unreliable, no one wants to take a chance on you. Virgil got Andre and I on the phone one night and I asked him to level with me. Andre's father had recently passed away and the grief was weighing on him. "He was my mother and my father and I'm really struggling with it," he explained. I knew Andre. I'd dealt with young men like him my entire life. And I knew that what he needed more than anything was a team he could trust and someone to show him the possibilities.

I flew Andre to Houston so I could see him in action for myself, and the boy truly had a gift. Roy Jones Jr. was his favorite boxer, so I took him to Roy's boxing camp in New Orleans. Roy watched Andre spar, and even he was impressed. Andre was inspired. Many times, kids with big dreams become intimidated by the distance between where they are and where they want to be. And once a child is intimidated, it's easy for them to get distracted. For Andre, the streets were a welcome distraction. Since he was nine years old, he lived a disciplined life. His father raised him as a boxer with a rigid schedule. Now that his father was gone, Andre was getting distracted. That kind of freedom isn't free. It's fun for a while, but rarely will anything come of it. It's easy to get caught up in the undisciplined life and before you know it, opportunities will pass you by. I told Andre if he would commit himself 100% to boxing, I would make sure he and his family were taken care of. I needed Andre to trust me, as his manager and as a man of my word.

After New Orleans, I flew Andre to Las Vegas to spar with Winky Wright. It was like magic watching Andre take Winky's jab away from him. By the third round, Winky declared that Andre was going to be a champion. Virgil made good on his promise to me in 2004 when Andre won the Olympic gold medal in Athens, Greece. I couldn't have been more proud. Andre was the first American boxer to win gold in eight years. Everyone wanted to sign him, but just as I'd stayed true to my word, Andre honored his and flew to Houston to sign his management agreement.

Over the years, Andre and I bonded over our love for boxing, and also our spirituality. Andre had strengthened his relationship with God while grieving the loss of his father, and faith was something that brought us closer together. This would prove valuable when we hit a rough patch six years later.

By 2010, Andre was unhappy with his contract terms. His contract was nearing completion, but although we talked about renegotiating, I wasn't willing to agree to the terms he was asking for. I knew I'd put together some very lucrative opportunities for Andre. Apparently he felt differently and filed a lawsuit against me. I called him a few days after I'd been served to try to get to the bottom of this, but we were still at a standstill, so I filed a countersuit against him.

This wasn't the first time I found myself locked in a legal battle with a client. But Andre was also a friend, someone I'd watched grow into a man. We were family and brothers in faith. As our lawyers prepared our cases, it didn't sit right with me. I saw it like this: I'd invested in Andre because I believe in him. And now that he was growing into his own, he expected me to reap less benefits. It felt like a slap in the face. I believe in doing good business, but you can never mistake business for personal. But on this rare occasion, it *was* personal. I wanted to try mediation; not with our attorneys but with our pastors.

Against the advice of my lawyers, my pastor Ralph West and I flew out to Oakland to meet with Andre and his pastor, Napoleon Kaufman, at The Well Christian Community Church in Livermore. The four of us gathered in Kaufman's office and went to work hammering out the differences between us. I understood then that Andre wasn't trying to cut me out or disrespect what we built together. He was trying to take control of his own destiny, and I could respect that. Four hours later we emerged with a new contract, and we both dropped our lawsuits. In the end, it wasn't one-sided. We compromised, and we're still moving forward together today. To find success, you have to know your craft, know your skill, and know your faith.

HOW DO I GET ON?

During the many years since the success of Rap-A-Lot, I've been approached by hundreds of aspiring record industry executives, producers, managers and artists all wanting to know the same thing: *how do I get on?*

Anyone who tries to sell you a specific formula as the definitive route to success in entertainment is lying. There is no *one* way to get on. My route to the top was a self-funded, grassroots exercise in trial and error. Lyor Cohen's rise began when Russell Simmons hired him. L.A. Reid began as an artist and transitioned into the boardroom. Roc-A-Fella started because Jay-Z needed a label that could support his own music. Each person's success is as individual as his or her own talent and resources. But once you accept that idea and take the challenge of using your own gifts and resources, there are some basic fundamental things you should have.

For one, a good lawyer is the difference between being paid for your work and watching someone else get paid for your work. On the streets, your freedom often depends on your legal representation. Once you found a good lawyer who understands your needs, you'd hold onto him or her. Even if you have to downsize and sell off everything you have, your lawyer is the very last thing you'd let go of. So when I went into the music business, I knew I'd need an attorney who understood my movement and my own specific challenges that I would face being in Houston, so far removed from New York and Los Angeles. And most importantly, I needed a lawyer who could anticipate what I would need as I grew, or what I'd need if growth wasn't happening as fast as it should. Even to this very day, I make determinations about how serious someone is based on the lawyer they bring to the table.

Just as important as a quality lawyer is a top-notch producer who knows how to make great music and spot great talent but also understands your movement, supports your movement, and will ride for your movement, no matter what. That last part is the hardest and most important part to find. There are millions of people who make beats, thousands who can put together an entire song, and hundreds who have a keen ear for a great artist. But it's difficult to find one who not only understands you but believes in you. And that belief is everything. When I came out of the streets and was spending all night in the studio, not knowing when or where we were going to make a profit, I needed my producer to be right there with me, every night. If your producer isn't passionate enough to give it 1,000% every single night, your product will suffer, and you won't have good quality music to market. Rick Rubin had to be dedicated to creating the music that Russell Simmons sold. Dr. Dre defined Death Row Records and Aftermath. The Medicine Men (formerly known as Beats By The Pound) gave No Limit the sound that made them famous. Mannie Fresh was the creative spine of Cash Money Records. A dedicated producer that's in it for the long haul is more important than gold.

For Rap-A-Lot, those producers were Bido and Mike Dean. Mike was a white boy who only knew how to play a few instruments when he came to me, but he had an amazing work ethic and the heart of a lion. He had a gift, and was willing to follow my lead. I helped create a lifestyle for him where he could always be accessible to me whenever I needed him, any hour of the day. Together, we were able to develop the Rap-A-Lot sound. I also put him in situations working under great producers like Dr. Dre and many others so he could learn their secrets and soak up game. Today, he works with Jay-Z and Kanye West as a producer and engineer. He's a one-man show for Kanye's whole fuckin' concert, he's the sound engineer and plays the instruments. So what I built in him is still relevant today in a major way.

Once you have your ride-or-die producer and a masterful attorney, you need the largest piece of the puzzle: a superstar.

My son Jas always had an interest in music. Like my other children, I didn't allow him to listen to Hip Hop in the house. And like my other children, he found a way to immerse himself in it anyway. By the time he turned twenty, Jas was already deep into the culture. While making his own music, he connected with many other young artists.

At its height, MySpace was an online hub where people from all over the world could meet. It was a useful platform for up-and-coming artists looking to take their local fan base international. Jas, like many people his age, had mastered social networking and would spend hours every day making new friends, meeting new fans and new artists. He clicked on hundreds of MySpace Music pages, listening to song snippets, counting fan follows, and watching videos, all in search of one thing: *buzz*.

A *buzz* can only be described as the undeniable conversation around an artist or a song. It's excitement, movement; a natural blend. The average person will never remember the second time they heard a song but most of us can never forget the first. Your first encounter with something *special* stirs your feelings and emotions. And the trained mind can discern what's special, even if they don't like it. The very first time I heard "Ice Ice Baby," I knew it would make money. There was an *it* factor that made the song interesting and infectious, but I still had my own opinion. And that's the mark of true art: does it make you *feel* something? Then once you've found something special and weighed in on it, the only thing left to do is share it. The very moment you feel compelled to say, "Hey, listen to this," a buzz is born.

I tell every young mogul, producer, and A&R that instead of searching for an artist, they should always look for talent, work ethic, and buzz. The first two without the last one is the difference between making music as a hobby and making music for the entire world.

Jas called me one day, excited. He was still figuring out his place within the music industry but felt he had a good eye and ear for talent. And he'd finally found someone he wanted to share with me. Jas came across a young artist from Toronto, Canada. He reached out and told the young artist he liked what he heard and could play his music for

Lil Wayne.

But first, he had to get me on board. I don't recall the exact song he played for me, but I remember that I didn't like it. The boy was rapping *and* singing, which didn't make sense to me. Sure, it was common for Rap-A-Lot rappers to sing his own hook, but it was always in the same tone as he delivered his rhymes. This boy was singing a melody. I didn't know what to make of it. But Jas reminded me of the lesson I always tried to teach him: learn to spot the buzz. This artist was buzzing, with two mixtapes under his belt and several thousand fans on MySpace. My son insisted there was something there. I asked him, "You like this?" and Jas said, "Yeah, dad, this is the new sound, by the way, he's buzzing!" My ears stuck up like a German Shepherd. I had some friends in Canada and I called them to ask if they'd heard of this artist named Drake. Their response was that he was the truth out there, so we flew him out.

At the time, it was school break and Jas was on tour with Lil Wayne. But I never wanted my son to be one of those guys just hanging around. If he was going to be out on the road, he needed to have a purpose. Jas wanted to start his own label, and he felt that this boy from Toronto should be his first artist. So I told Jas to tell Wayne that his father was going to give him a million dollars to start his own label and that he had an artist he wanted Wayne to meet.

Like me, Wayne wasn't feeling Drake's music when he first heard it either. But Jas kept at it, sending beats to Canada and then playing the finished tracks for Wayne whenever he got a chance. Finally, Jas got his hands on the "A Milli" beat. It was the hottest song in the country and Jas wasn't even supposed to have the instrumental. He sent it to Drake and had him lay down his verse. Then he played it for Wayne. It worked. They brought Drake down to Houston and he joined them on tour.

You can't listen to the first "no." Many times you can't listen to "no" at all. If you believe that something will work, you have to keep working at it until you become right. Jas knew the buzz on Drake was real when neither Wayne or I saw it. And he kept pushing. That's the important part: keep pushing. But he was smart about it. He didn't keep coming back with the same song. He tried different ways until he found one that stuck. That's what a businessman does: he keeps working on his product until he gets something that's good enough to sell.

Now that Wayne was sold, things quickly moved for Drake. He began work on what would become *So Far Gone*, a mixtape so good it was nominated for a Grammy. The music he began making was special. He had his own style that even I started to appreciate.

It's funny looking back on it, because now I think Drake's one of the best. *So Far Gone* took Drake's buzz to an all-out frenzy and suddenly everyone wanted to sign him, but Jas and I already made an agreement. Cortez Bryant, or just "Tez," is Lil Wayne's friend and longtime manager. He saw what Wayne saw: Drake was going to be a star. He and Wayne decided to come in as partners with Jas and I, in signing Drake to Wayne's label, Young Money, which was a subsidiary of Cash Money. At the time, everyone involved was traveling all over the country. Tez flew to Houston to sit down and hammer out how we were all going to be part of the new team forming around Drake. But aside from that, most of our other communications had been informal conversations over the phone.

That's how most of the entertainment business works. Someone comes up with an idea, reaches out to someone to bring it to life, and then attorneys come in and make it official. But things got complicated because Drake was rising so quickly. He wasn't some artist we were planning to *begin* working with; he was already selling music and performing shows. So we made many of the earlier decisions based on trust that everyone would keep their word. But it's important to always get it in writing.

"I just found out today that your son is the one who discovered Drake," Mike Kyser, the President of Urban Music at Atlantic Records, laughed into the phone. "But when I heard that, my question was, 'Then where is J. Prince in all of this?'"

"Here I am, live and in living color," I replied. I'd called Mike to find out about Gee Roberson. At the time, Gee was the VP of A&R at Atlantic Records. He was at the forefront of the bidding war to sign Drake, and he'd never consulted me. In fact, Gee said he had no idea I was even involved. Gee was also a partner in Hip Hop Since 1978, a very successful management company that managed Lil Wayne and several other high-profile rappers. And now he was somehow managing Drake. There's a funny story how that happened.

After Tez's initial visit to Houston, Jas and I was left with the understanding that we would split the recording contract with Tez and Wayne, 50/50. However, Tez had been slow in drawing up a contract.

I'd reached out several times, checking in to make sure our agreement was being honored, but apparently, it wasn't.

Jas had been kicked off Wayne's tour for no apparent reason. He'd simply been booked on a flight home to Houston, and neither of us could get Tez on the phone. That's always a red flag. When someone starts avoiding you, know that things are about to change. So I told Jas to meet me in Las Vegas, where Wayne's tour was headed. After the show, I spoke with Tez backstage. As expected, he assured me that everything was being honored and the contracts were forthcoming.

I told him to come to Houston and explain to me exactly what was going on. Shortly after, Tez came down to talk and said that Drake was the hold up; he was having an issue with my son's name on the contract. Tez assured me that no matter what company name appeared, he had every intention of honoring our verbal agreement.

After that meeting, Tez stopped returning my calls, so I reached out to Baby and Slim at Cash Money. We'd always had a good rapport and I knew I could get a straight answer out of them. Slim told me that Gee Roberson was now calling the shots where Drake was concerned. I'd never even heard of Gee, but apparently, he'd been put in place as management.

"I heard you're the mastermind trying to screw me." It was my first conversation with Gee, and I wasted no time getting right to the point. He assured me that wasn't the case; he said he respected me and my contributions to the culture, and was unaware that my son and I were even involved in the Drake situation. I couldn't tell if he was lying to me or not. But the more Gee began to walk me through his involvement, it became clear he wasn't the thief. When you call someone out, you have to allow them the opportunity to explain. There's something to be said about a man who can be straight up when you're applying pressure. And I felt that Gee was being straight with me. So I put together a meeting to get to the bottom of things.

During the 2012 BET Awards in Los Angeles, we all met at a hotel: Jas, Gee, Tez, Baby, Slim. Instantly, I put Tez under the spotlight. Our initial agreement, which wasn't being honored, was with him. As he discussed that agreement, he left out key elements. At this point I realized that there had been a lot of mixed messages, and it was obvious who the messenger was. I wasn't going to stand for any more disrespect. I gave him one more chance to explain the agreement to everyone in the room, but it became obvious that I was dealing with an amateur. He had been the person failing to communicate all along.

I asked Baby and Slim to leave. This was an issue between Gee, Tez and I. A few minutes later as they cleared out of the room, Gee asked if he could speak with Tez privately, so I obliged. They returned to the room 15 minutes later, asking what would it take to make this situation right. We agreed to the terms, the contract was drawn up shortly thereafter, and everyone kept their word.

LIL WAYNE & CASH MONEY

THE ART & SCIENCE OF
respect

Bryan "Baby/Birdman" Williams and Ronald "Slim" Williams were two young guys out of New Orleans, trying to do the same thing for their city that I'd done for mine. They first reached out to me in the early 1990s. Rap-A-Lot had put Houston on the map and they wanted to do the same for their city. I liked how consistent they were. The two brothers paid close attention to detail and they were defining their own style of music. I tried to help them any way I could. I became their OG and considered them my brothers in this game. That's why I didn't think twice about sending my son Jas out on the road with their artist Lil Wayne. At the time, Jas was still in college. I'm a man who's big on respect and trust, so for me to allow my son to travel with them showed my level of trust and respect for the Cash Money family.

When Drake was buzzing, I could've taken him to Jay-Z for a deal. Lyor Cohen would've taken him. Or I could've signed him to the home team and made him a Rap-A-Lot artist, but I didn't. Instead I told Jas to go talk to Wayne about him. Why? Because they were family. And family eats at home.

After the meeting in Los Angeles, Drake made some changes to his camp and Gee Roberson and Tez were removed. We got a better idea of the amount of money that was owed and the concern then became recouping our share of earnings. To date, Drake continues to be one of the most successful artists of his generation. He's sold a lot of records, sold out arenas, and continues to grow. Cash Money has made a lot of money from an artist we all share. Although money was being made, we never received proper financial statements or checks even though our contract as partners in this profit share was clear. They were blatantly breaching our agreement and they needed to pay up. It was disrespectful for them to have the audacity to not pay my son.

Everybody's heard rumblings about Cash Money's reputation for not paying people they owe, but knowing the relationship we had, I never once considered that. Once it was determined they owed us several million dollars in back earnings, I asked Baby to make a "good faith" payment. He said they needed extra time to prepare the financial statements, which would clearly show the amount that was (and still is) owed. Right before Christmas of 2012, he hit me off a million dollars and assured me that he hadn't forgotten about my son, but he still owed us several million dollars. So I asked for another good faith payment with the understanding that I shouldn't have to ask anymore. Another several months went by. A show of "good faith" only works if you're showing "good faith." And all of this time, Drake was continuing to earn money that they alone were pocketing. So I hit Baby up again. He always answered the phone right away. Again, he assured me he hadn't forgotten about me or my son, and he hit me off with another million dollars. It was at that point that I told him, "Look, I don't want my money spoon-fed to me. Pay *all* of what you owe me."

That's when things got uncomfortable. I suggested that we audit the amount of money owed to us, which led to Jas, myself and my accountant going to New York to look through the books. We found plenty of discrepancies, which ultimately has led to a full-blown ongoing lawsuit.

I will end this simply by saying that I will not allow Cash Money, Baby nor Slim to take anything from me or my son. As I said on my "Courtesy Call": "Do right by me."

My relationship with Lil Wayne is a different matter. Of course I met Wayne through Baby and Slim, embracing him as Baby's son, showing him all the love I'd shown Baby and Slim. For years our relationship had been amicable. If Wayne ever needed anything, I was right there, and he showed that love right back to me. In 2008, he came out to my ranch and did a photo shoot for my condom company Strapped for free. He'd make guest appearances on Rap-A-Lot songs and never asked for a dime, because that was our relationship. He was the son of family, which made him family. I was taught that family shouldn't disrespect each other, especially not in public.

The rift between Wayne and my son began years ago when Jas was put off the tour, while Drake was kept on. And it grew from there. But I've never concerned myself with that Easy-Bake Oven beef.

Out of nowhere the vibe changed and Jas never went on the second tour. There's something that exists with a lot of guys who are in a powerful position. They try to dominate situations with other powerful men instead of collaborating and combining their power. If you're in their space and you're still shining, still have your swag, and you're not submitting to their crazy-ass domination tactics, they create more shit and it gets foul. That's how it was for me on the block when I was growing up; somebody would constantly want to fuck with me over and over again. They'll size you up, from the girls you date to your swagger. When they see that you got it, shit ends up boiling inside of them as you continue building your credibility. So as a father, being in tune with what's going on, I see shit like this all the time. It's not just with me, but even where my sons are concerned.

Still, Jas is a grown man and can fight his own battles. So even throughout our legal dispute with Cash Money, I didn't feel negative towards Lil Wayne until I heard him say, "You need a king, fuck the Prince." Whatever has happened between Jas and Wayne has always been a problem between them. But when you include my family name in your insults – over a girl – you've crossed a line with me.

The best part about this story is that time allowed wounds to heal and didn't allow us to cross paths. By the time we met, Lil Wayne's respect for me had overcome my anger towards him. I realized that he and my son were victims of the same circumstances. The bigger picture is for us to stick together on one accord to fight the enemy who thinks they are invincible.

HEART, LOYALTY, & COMMITMENT

As I look back on my foundation of Rap-A-Lot, I built my team around three ingredients: heart, loyalty, and commitment. In my journey, those three character qualities have proven to be more important than a degree, experience, or other qualifications.

Someone who has "heart" is a stand-up guy. (Or girl.) You can't punk them. You can't put fear in them. A loyal person has my back, even when I'm not looking. They're gonna be real with me and tell me the truth, even when it's not popular. And a committed person is someone who's going to be there in the rain, sleet, or snow. They don't make a lot of excuses; they do everything in their power to get the job done. They're gonna be there on time, and they're not looking at the clock all day in a rush to leave.

I also hired people at Rap-A-Lot with college degrees, so I definitely don't discredit education. I also don't discredit someone with experience and a proven track record. But to me, those are secondary. Heart, loyalty, and commitment comes first. I took people with those three ingredients and put them to work under more educated people. As they continued to learn, they became even more valuable.

I'm not afraid of giving an ex-convict a second chance as long as they are serious about changing their life. Rap-A-Lot was successful with a team of ex-convicts, people who America would say doesn't deserve a second chance. Some of my homies just wanted an opportunity. If they were 100% committed, I would embrace them with the understanding that they couldn't straddle the fence. That meant they couldn't be working at Rap-A-Lot if they still had an illegal hustle on the side which could contaminate my movement. That was always clear and understood, and monitored to a certain extent. Just because you're given an opportunity doesn't mean that you're going to be wide open, free to do whatever you wanna do. I had a system in place. You're gonna be policed by another homie, and in order for you to grow, you have to earn the position. For example, I mentioned Mike Mack in an earlier chapter. He started out making $150/week and grew to a half a million dollar salary. I hired a three-time convicted felon named Carlton Joshua and put him to work under Mike Mack. Carlton proved himself to be worthy of the position and worked his way up to a $250,000 salary.

Some of Rap-A-Lot's biggest assets were street guys. I think they're some of the most brilliant people in the world once they've made their mind up to compete in corporate America. I tell all of them, "You have no idea how brilliant you are." They just have to apply the same energy that they're applying in the streets. They have a lot of advantages and don't even know it. They haven't been brainwashed by the system, so their risk tolerance is higher.

It definitely takes a gift to recognize people with heart, loyalty, and commitment. I do have a gift of intuition and discernment, and I was raised in the hood, so I know how to recognize bullshit. I just need about 20 or 30 minutes in someone's presence and I'll be able to get a feel for their capabilities. I'm going to search them without even putting a hand on them. A wise man is quick to listen and slow to speak. A person will tell you everything you need to know about them if you listen and have the patience to hear them out. That's why I love listening. I give them respect and hear them out, and I'm calculating things as I listen.

To me, trust is something that has to be earned. I gave a lot of people the opportunity, and everybody didn't make it. Here's one example of someone who was given an opportunity and wasn't worthy. I had several guys working as security overnight at the Rap-A-Lot compound, and some money came up missing from my sister's office.

Once I learned there was a rat in the building, I set a trap with hidden security cameras. Then I put cheese in the trap – I left a couple hundred dollars on my sister's desk. The rat went for it.

So I had a meeting. I brought in three security guards and explained that money was missing. I said, "One of you has taken something from me. I'ma give you an opportunity to square up. If you square up with me, I'ma look at you with more respect."

I believe that a man who can admit when he's wrong is someone you can halfway trust moving forward. But a man who continues lying can't be trusted, and has to be dealt with accordingly.

So I asked the first guy, "Did you take that money off the desk?" He said, "Naw, I ain't done nothing like that to you, boss. I wouldn't do that." I asked the second man, "Was it you? Did you go into the office and take that money?" He said, "Naw, you kept it real with me for too long. I wouldn't do nothing like that." I asked the third man, and he denied it too. "Man, you took care of me the whole time I was in the penitentiary," he said. He swore up and down on his mother and father that he would never take anything from me.

Understand, I already knew who it was. The third man, the one who was doing all of the swearing, was the guilty party. I played the security footage for him and let him see himself. The situation was handled and he lost the privilege of working in that building.

Overall, though, most of the people I believed in proved to be worthy of the opportunity. My friend Anthony has one of the biggest hearts I've ever witnessed in a man. He was the one who was busted with 76 kilos in the 1980s. Law enforcement offered him his freedom – all he had to do was lie and say that the kilos belonged to me. His heart was so big, his loyalty was so strong, and his commitment was so over-whelming that he wouldn't do that. Years later, when the DEA was at-tacking me, agents Jack Schumacher and Chad Scott set a trap for two of my employees. My friend Big Steve was arrested, and a DEA agent came to talk to him. He told them, "You can have your mammy come in here and give me head through these bars and I still ain't gonna tell no lie on that man."

And last but not least, my homie Big Chief was one of the first to exer-cise his heart, loyalty, and commitment by quitting his high-paying job to come work by my side. He put in countless hours traveling around the world with my artists and accomplishing every mission that was assigned to him. He dealt with large amounts of money and was never a penny short.

Throughout my life these are the kind of people I've surrounded myself with. I look for individuals with heart, loyalty, and commitment. That's my advice to everybody who's building a team. When you're committed to something, you believe in it so strongly you're willing to die for it. And anybody who doesn't have something worth dying for isn't really living.

212-274-0464   JESTINE 324-5440

THINGS TO DO

1. GET 32 ALBUM DONE
2. CHECK ON BUSHWICK AND SHAD SONG
* 3. CLOSE DANA DEAL WITH MAVERICK
* 4. PUBLISHING DEAL WITH EMI
* 5. CUT STAFF AT RAP-A-LOT
* 6 GET PAYMENT FROM RICK RUBEN
* 7. TRY TO WORK A DEAL ON GETO BOYS MASTERS R
8 BUILD VERA A HOUSE
* 9. GET WITH JOE CANTU ON MONEY IN BANK
* 10. CLOSE DEAL WITH SUAVE RRCORDS EIGHT BALL
11. MAKE JOHN OFFER ON BUYING STUDIO
12 CHECK ON BUILDING MYOWN STUDIO
* 13 BUY BIDO A VAN   OR LEXUS
* 14 SEE IF BUSHWICK OR CHIEF WANT TRUCK
* 15. BREAK OFF MONEY TO HOMIES
16 START MY MOTHER A ACCOUNT IN BANK
MARTY *17 TALK TO BRUCE ABOUT HIS SITUATION
*BANDIER 18 ASK KEN BERRY ABOUT EMI PUBL. GUY
* 19 ASK KEN A BOUT ADVANCE ON FACE ANDBUSHWICK
* 20 WHAT HAPPEND WITH WILLIED LAWYER
* 21 CHECK WITH CJ ON BUSHWICK
* 22 BRUCE CALL MARK
* 23 GET PHONE FROM KEVIN CALL CHIEF
* 24 ASK MARK ABOUT MY CHECK

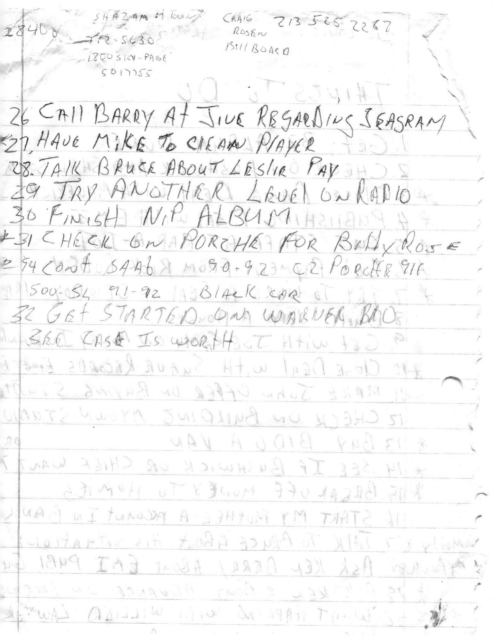

As you can see, this is confirmation of the importance of writing a to-do list and following through on it. Here's one of my to-do lists from 1994.

PERSONAL GOALS

I accomplished all the ten goals I'd written out for myself. But you can only get so much satisfaction out of doing things for yourself. I got the most joy from giving back to the people who had played a special role in my life. In 1993, I made a list of personal goals; things I wanted to provide for the people who were close to me.

Some people become successful and never think about doing something for somebody else. You gotta have a different perspective of what to do with your riches. Don't make it all about yourself.

From the beginning, my objective to break the poverty curse in my family wasn't for me. It was for my mother. I sacrificed for a long time. I drove around in a raggedy truck and didn't buy anything for myself until I was able to buy my mother her first house with an acre of land. Just imagine: I was willing to die for my mother to have that house. But I lived, and was still able to get her the house, and go above and beyond for her. Witnessing the smile on her face - the woman who gave birth to me – that moment meant more to me than any amount of money.

I built my grandmother a two-story brick home, her dream house, in our hood. It sticks out like a sore thumb in the Fifth Ward, but it's a beautiful thing for the kids there to see. It's something to inspire them. When I walked to school as a kid, I'd only see one or two brick houses in the neighborhood, but that was enough to give me the dream of owning one someday.

I didn't really know my biological father Ernest Prince until I was an adult. A lot of people advised me not to do anything for him; they said he hadn't done anything for me. I disagree. Both he and my mother gave me life, so I didn't hold the past against him. I loved him at the age I met him, and we were able to spend a lot of quality time together. Among the many things I was able to do for him, I did purchase a new home and lots of nice vehicles.

After my father Adam Hackett passed, I supported my stepmother, Patricia Hackett. I was able to be there for her in a variety of ways and bring joy to her life. I paid off her house and bought her new vehicles. I purchased a house with a few acres of land for my other stepfather, Henry Martin, and a variety of trucks for him. I was able to build a home and a cabin and purchase vehicles for my grandmother Nano, Ernest's mother. She's 98 years old now. 'Til this very day, I am there for them in any capacity that's needed. I help them meet the needs they have on a daily / monthly basis. I was able to alleviate many major financial stressors of life for them, so they could concentrate on doing what they really want to do instead of what they have to do in order to live. I feel now it's my turn to contribute to take care of them.

Of course, all of my children were on my goal list. It was very important to me to give my children a major jump start in life and help them become whatever they wanted to be. I purchased homes and vehicles for my children and sent them to college.

Don't misunderstand me, though – my children weren't spoiled. I provided them with material things, but I also taught them respect. Even though I had housekeepers, I'd stop the housekeepers from doing everything for them like making the children's beds and cleaning their rooms. I wanted them to learn how to be responsible and clean up after themselves instead of having someone else do it for them all of the time. That was part of the structure that existed in my house. I didn't just talk to my children about work; I allowed them to witness my work. I believe more is caught then taught, so I was an example by action. Christmas in my household was more about giving than receiving. I'd take them to feed the homeless and put more emphasis on that instead of just gifts they're receiving.

I didn't even allow rap music to enter my home for a long time because I didn't want rap music raising my children. I understand how strong it can be, so I had to control it. Even though we built Rap-A-Lot into a successful company, everyone has a choice what to allow or not to allow in their household. There's a time and a place for everything, and I didn't feel that it was appropriate for my children to have access to R-rated movies or uncensored rap too soon. When I was a child, I had access to everything, and I understood what it did to me. It matured me way beyond my years.

Of course, by the time my children hit high school and started driving their own cars, yeah, they were jamming rap music. But before then, as a parent, I felt that it was my responsibility to protect their minds and their hearts until they were mature enough to really dissect and digest it.

Aside from my blood relatives, there were friends on my goal list too. It's all about loyalty and love. When my friend NC was killed, his son was just a baby. I bought a new home and vehicle for NC's girlfriend, helped raised his son and put him through school. I still contribute to them on a monthly basis. While my friend Anthony was in the penitentiary for 18 years, I made sure his family was good. I bought him a new home and looked out for his children until he came home.

All these people on my goal list were some of many who were loyal to me and showed me love. Being the person that I am, I had to do the same thing in return. Over the years it's been a blessing and a curse. If I embrace a person as family, then I'm down with them through the sunshine and the rain. I'm just built that way.

I was blessed to be able to give back to these and others who contributed to my life in some significant way. Now I'm in a position to take care of them because they took care of me. That's the ultimate high for me; I don't even need drugs. There's no better joy to me, than becoming a blessing to a person who contributed to my journey. I witnessed great examples of people who had big hearts and gave, throughout my life. I believe that to whom much is given, much is required. Knowing that called me to give on another level, with structure.

Some people are just born with the heart to fulfill needs and help, I guess. For me, I consider it a privilege and an honor to be chosen to complete such a task for so many. I walk in great respect for universal laws. From childhood I moved in a way before I could even understand what these laws were, but I over-stood sowing and reaping, planting seeds in fertile grounds, focusing on and attracting what you want, speaking things into existence, watching and respecting nature, walking in abundance and gifting others. No one owes anyone anything, that's the thing. I never felt obligated to care for my family or friends, I just give from the heart out of love.

ACKNOWLEDGMENTS

First of all, I would like to thank my mother for giving me a chance at life. I know it wasn't easy for a sixteen-year-old single mom to survive in the 1960s. I love and appreciate everything you've done for me, because I know you gave your best. I was paying attention when you spoke. I heard your cries and witnessed your work ethic. Even though you fell short financially of reaching your goal of buying a home, your love was sufficient, and that's what gave me the desire. I was willing to die for you to have that house. I hope I make you proud to be my mother. Love you.

A special thanks to my grandmother Vera. I was so blessed to witness a hard-working woman who would give you the shirt off her back. Thanks for being an example of unconditional love and loving me as if I was your own child. When my sister Zenia passed away at the age of twelve, a piece of me died with her, and it was you who nurtured me back to life. I'm forever grateful for those memories and many more where you protected me from hurt, harm and danger. I love you for life!

To my mother Pat, who never gave up on me no matter what I did. You were always there with open arms and that beautiful smile. I never witnessed the type of love you shared with me. Even when I was dead wrong, you encouraged me by making me give my word to "never do it again," which was more effective than traditional discipline. Thank you for showing me the qualities of a virtuous woman. I was watching when you were carrying the load by yourself for the whole family. All I would say to myself is, *I want a wife like Pat someday*. Love you Pat!

To the matriarch, the miracle lady that God has blessed to live 98 years, my God-fearing grandmother Nano. What a blessing it is to witness a living miracle; still driving and functioning in full capacity at your age. It's such an honor to be your grandson for so many reasons, but the one that sticks out the most is your love for God. Thank you for every example of truth you've shared with our family and friends! You're the best example of a human being I've ever met. Love you!

To my sister Ronda who works diligently 24/7 at any hour, anywhere, without any complaints. I'm proud of who you have become in the business world and I'm also proud to call you my sister. Prior to our dad passing, I asked him if he thought Ronda could handle the load of working in entertainment. Days went by without him giving me an answer. On the last day I saw him alive, he said to me, "That question you asked me about Ronda... She can handle it." He was absolutely right! She's got my back and I have hers, even after death.

To Mary, thank you for the years of loyalty and dedication to our family. I thank God for the great memories and the unconditional love you've shared with all of us.

In loving memory of Adam, who first taught me what manhood was all about. I'm forever grateful to him for instilling the principles of respect, structure and discipline in my life. Even though I didn't appreciate it at the time, I could not be the man I am today without those lessons. He died at the tender age of 44 years old, but the lessons he taught still live in me today.

To one of the biggest-hearted men I know, my dad Henry. What a delight it was, and still is, to have this man in my life. He taught me by example how to work hard, and the importance of giving and spirituality. Henry, better known as "Ironman Martin," is a welder by trade, and he worked me like a grown man when I was a kid. It was that work ethic that shaped and molded me into the relentless hard worker that I am today. There was never a moment where he made me feel as though I was not his biological son. In his house, he was always OUR daddy. I am forever grateful for those memories.

In memory of Ernest Prince III, my biological father. A lot of people never knew why I changed my name from Smith to Prince. It's because I was a Prince the whole time. I didn't know who my biological father was until I was 17 or 18 years old. But the day I met the Prince side of my family, it was the beginning of the fulfillment of a void that had been empty in me all of my life. When I was able to see the truth, and see myself in my Prince family members, it was an eye-opening moment. I saw and felt my roots. Ernest was one of the wisest men I ever met. He shone a light on many of my gifts that I'd been unaware of.

He taught me the power of thinking and using my mind to conquer situations. Again, I couldn't be the man I am today without the final touches that he added to my life. Long live the Prince!

To my children: Ashley, Nicoi, James, Jas, Andre, Maya and Jay, I'm thankful for the days each of you were born. Life wouldn't be as flavorful without you. I'm proud of each of you and what you've accomplished thus far. I hope you value who you are and what you represent as much as I do. Just know it's an honor and a privilege to be your father. I love you.

To all my Family and my Friends who have contributed to my life personally and in business, there are far too many of you to name, but please understand that I have engraved all of your names in my heart. I appreciate every one of you because I couldn't have made it without you. This has been, and still is, a beautiful journey and I am forever grateful that God allowed our paths to cross. Thanks to all of you who have unending love for me.

And last but not least, to the listeners and readers of this book, I hope you enjoyed me sharing some of my life experiences with you and I hope you apply some of my wisdom to your life. It worked for me and many others.

The race is not given to the swift nor the strong, but unto them that endure to the end. - Ecclesiastes 9:11

EPILOGUE

You know, I've never been big on talking. I'm about action. And it's a heck of a thing to detail your life as I've done in this book. I've had to revisit people, places, moments that I've forgotten about, despite how they've changed me. During this process I went back to the Coke apartments, which for me is a regular thing. But on this particular day in August of 2014, I went inside my old apartment and stood in my childhood bedroom for the first time since shortly after my sister's death. If you'd asked me then if I could see myself where I am now – a Hip Hop legend, an influential boxing manager, and one of the most polarizing figures in American politics – I would've told you yes and no.

As a child, growing up in the Fifth Ward, there was no way I could've guessed that I would live the life that I have now. No two days are the same. I travel the world 40 weeks out of the year, working on numerous business ventures ranging from entertainment to agriculture.

My phones are my office, keeping me connected to partners and clients all over the globe. My children have choices in life that I never thought were possible. As I watch them grow into adulthood, I'm reminded of one thing I did know: I could do anything. I knew from a young age that there was an anointing on my life and that I was meant for great things. There were so many basic necessities that I didn't have. But one thing I did have was hope. And that's why I wrote this book.

I didn't set out to make history. I started with one tangible idea that I was passionate about - to break my family's cycle of poverty. And I believed in it so much that I was willing to die for it. But it was that passion, that unwavering belief in God's divine plan for my life, that made the difference between giving up and sticking it out when things got rough and it looked like there was no way out.

In the future, I plan to release a movie about my life. Other than that, I really don't want people to know what I'm going to do. They gotta wait and see.

Every day I'm approached by young aspiring music executives, artists, athletes and guys in the hood just looking for a way out. And I see so much of myself in many of them. But the difference between the ones that make it and the ones that don't isn't just talent, relationships, or even effort. It's faith. I wanted these pages in this book to show that all of my life someone has tried to tell me what I couldn't do, what I couldn't have and who I couldn't become. And it's always been up to me to say, "No. I'm bound for greatness because God said so." That's what made me unstoppable. That's what made me successful. That's what made me the one and only J. Prince.

GOAL SET

I WANT TO PAY OFF ALL MY BALANCES ON EVERYTHING I OWN IN 1993

WHAT	WHEN	HOW MUCH
* 1. B HOUSE	BY JUNE 93	63,526.57
* 2. B CAR	BY JUNE 93	2,649.84
* 3. V CAR -4	BY JUNE 93	16,960.35
* 4. M HOUSE	BY JUNE 93	252,776.09
5. LEXUS		
* 6. TRUCK	BY JUNE 93	23,500.00
* 7. P HOUSE	BY MARCH 93	~~36,000.00~~
* 8. N VAN	BY JUNE 93	11,077.72
9.		
10.		
TOTAL		353,490.57

12
3,600
3

Writing down your goals, looking at them frequently, and taking action every day to accomplish them will make them a reality. Here are my goal lists from 1993.

GOAL SET

I WANT TO BECOME A MULTIMILLIONAIRE
OUTSIDE OF RAP-A-LOT ACCOUNT

HOW	WHEN
* GETO BOYS RELEASE	NEED BUDGET
* SCARFACE RELEASE	NEED BUDGET
* TMT RELEASE	NEED BUDGET
* GANGSTA NIP RELEASE	NEED BUDGET
* DANA DANE RELEASE	NEED BUDGET
* DMG RELEASE	NEED BUDGET
* TOO LOW RELEASE	NEED BUDGET
* FIFTH WARD BOYS	NEED BUDGET
* ODD SQUAD RELEASE	NEED BUDGET
* BIG MIKE RELEASE	NEED BUDGET
32 RELEASE	NEED BUDGET
* SEAGRAM RELEASE	NEED BUDGET
* MAKE	DISTRUBUTING DEALS

BUSINESS
GOALS   WHEN, WHERE, HOW.

* 1. I WANT TO PAY OFF ALL
MY BALANCES ON EVERY THING
I OWN,

* 2. I WANT TO PLACE A STRONG
TEAM AT RAP-A-LOT.

* 3. I WANT TO BECOME A MULTI Millionaire
~~#4~~ Outside of RAP-A-LOT'S Account

* 4 START NEW LABEL SING-A-LOT

* 5 START NEW JIMMY HAT COMPANY

6 START BONDING COMPANY

* 7. PUT AS MANY BROTHERS OFF
THE STREET TO WORK

8 HELP THE POOR BUSINESS PROP

9. MAKE A MOVIE ABOUT MY LIFE

* 10 BUY MY MOTHER A NOTHER HOME

WHEN
WHERE
HOW

GOAL SET   MAY 1. 1994

✱ 1. MORE MUSC⬤LIE IN RAP-A-LOT
RADIO, VIDEO, MARKETING, PUBLICITY

✱ 2. OVERSEAS DISTR. DEAL

✱ 3. BUY MY MOTHER A HOUSE

✱ 4 BAY PAT A CAR.

✱ 5 RESTRUCTURE RAP-A-LOT STAFF

✱ 6 PRAY EVERY MORNING

7 BUILD VERA A HOUSE

8 WORK OUT PUBLISHING DEAL WITH EMI

In addition to Business Goals, I set Personal Goals for
myself - things I wanted to do for family and friends who
had contributed to my life. I'm grateful that I've been able
to check off everything on both lists, with the exception of
"Make a Movie About My Life" - and that's coming soon.

When I was a kid, my grandma lived in these apartments. One day the rent man came knocking on the door and my grandma told me to say she wasn't there. So I went to the door and said, "My grandma says to tell you she's not here." Long story short, I got an ass-whupping for saying the wrong thing. And that day planted a seed in my mind that

one day I was going to buy those apartments so he wouldn't be bothering my grandmother anymore. Today, I own these apartments, and my grandmother owns a beautiful home. I also bought the laundromat attached to these apartments and renamed it after her, Vera's Washateria (pictured on page 7).